no easy answers

making good decisions in an anything-goes world

FAITH
ALIVE®
Christian Resources

Grand Rapids, Michigan

Cover art: The Image Bank

We are grateful to Dan VanderArk for writing the case studies for this course. A former high-school principal, Dan is executive director of Christian Schools International, Grand Rapids, Michigan. We also thank Bob Rozema for writing this leader's guide. Bob is a former editor for CRC Publications; he lives in Spring Lake, Michigan.

Faith Alive Christian Resources published by CRC Publications.
No Easy Answers: Making Decisions in an Anything-Goes World. Church school material for high school students, © 2002, CRC Publications, 2850 Kalamazoo Ave. SE, Grand Rapids, MI 49560. All rights reserved. Printed in the United States of America on recycled paper. ♻

We welcome your comments. Call us at 1-800-333-8300 or e-mail us at editors@faithaliveresources.org.

ISBN 1-56212-845-0

10 9 8 7 6 5 4 3 2 1

contents

how to use this course

Welcome to *No Easy Answers: Making Good Decisions in an Anything-Goes World.* If this brief overview doesn't answer all your questions, please feel free to call us at 1-800-333-8300 or e-mail us at editors@faithaliveresources.org. Thanks.

No Easy Answers is a practical, hands-on course on how to make Christian moral decisions. Leaders of our previous course on ethics—called *Decisions*—should know that this new course is much shorter than the old one (thirteen sessions instead of twenty-four) and uses new cases and teaching strategies.

Aimed at high school students, especially juniors and seniors and recent graduates, *No Easy Answers* features the use of case studies—true accounts of persons who have struggled with some kind of moral dilemma or problem. Such cases are effective because they involve students in interesting "real-life" issues, allow freedom of expression, and require supporting opinion with facts from the case and principles from God's Word.

In this course, you'll be teaching your students how to make moral choices according to Christian ethical principles in concrete life situations. You'll be helping them to form for themselves a Christian pattern of moral living, making decisions and taking actions that seek the glory of God, the good of neighbors, and personal well-being. These are ambitious and absolutely crucial goals, especially in the "anything goes" world teens encounter every day—in the sitcoms and movies they view, in the music they listen to, on the Web, among their classmates, on the job, and just about everywhere else.

In such a world, your teens need all the help they can get in making good choices and living as followers of Jesus Christ. This course aims to get them started on the road to making sound, Christian choices.

Organization

Two introductory sessions are followed by ten that are modeled after the Ten Commandments—the basic, biblical imperatives that express God's will for our moral choosing and doing. When seen in the light of Christ's fulfillment and obeyed in the freedom of the Spirit, these commandments become a useful catalog of basic ethical principles.

A concluding session encourages students to practice the ethical principles they've been studying. Leaders who want to stretch the course to more than thirteen sessions may use some of the alternate case studies provided for each commandment (in addition to the main case for each commandment).

Student Materials

Each student should receive a **packet of twenty case study cards** for sessions 3-12 on the Ten Commandments. Two cases are provided for each commandment—a main case and an alternate case. Use an alternate case if you prefer it to the main case or if you wish to expand the course to more than thirteen sessions.

It's important to give students only one case study card at a time. This prevents reading ahead, which robs the cases of their freshness and effectiveness. Between sessions, keep the case studies in your classroom or bring them home.

In addition to the case study cards, students will use **resource pages** that we ask you to photocopy from the back of this leader's guide. These provide a variety of resources you'll need to teach the sessions, including Bible passages, excerpts from the Heidelberg Catechism, and more.

Leader Materials

This leader's guide gives you detailed suggestions for teaching each session. Each session features

- **Focus:** Briefly describes the main idea or theme of the session.

- **Scripture:** Lists the passages used in the session.

- **Goals:** Summarizes what you and the students want to accomplish in the session.

- **Background:** Provides helpful insights into the content of the session. Written by the late Harvey A. Smit for the original *Decisions* course, these backgrounds have been updated with references to the cases and with other material written by Dr. Smit.

- **Session at a Glance:** Outlines each step of the session, the materials you need, and the approximate time each step requires (sessions are designed for 50-60 minutes).

- **Leading the Session:** Gives detailed directions for each step, including (for sessions 3-12) directions for teaching both the main case and the alternate case. Includes a number of options, activity adaptations, and tips.

We encourage you to modify the suggestions for leading the sessions to suit your own time frame, teaching style, and the needs of your students.

In addition to the leader's guide and case studies, you'll need Bibles, newsprint (preferably with an easel), markers, and notecards. Check the *materials* section for occasional additions to this list.

Evaluation

Evaluation forms are included for you and for your students at the back of this leader's guide. Please complete and send to

> *No Easy Answers*
> Faith Alive Christian Resources
> 2850 Kalamazoo Ave SE
> Grand Rapids, MI 49560

Thank you.

tips on teaching cases

Case studies are a great way to learn, as your students will soon discover. But it can take a little practice to get used to this method. Since many of the cases do not have a definite right or wrong answer, your role will be mainly that of helping students examine the question or issue.

What Are Case Studies?

Case studies are true accounts of persons who have struggled with some kind of moral dilemma or problem. Cases always call for a decision (from the students) that will end the dilemma or resolve the problem. For example, a Christian must decide if, in good conscience, she may participate in a non-Christian religious ritual. A teen must decide what to do with damaging information she has about a popular praise team leader. A young man must weigh the advantages and disadvantages of working on Sunday. A governor must decide whether or not to pardon a prisoner on death row who has recently become a strong Christian. A summer employee must decide whether or not to blow the whistle on his boss, who is cheating on the job. All these cases involve a problem that Christians could resolve in different ways.

You will notice that some of the case studies have a stronger dilemma or problem than others. In a few case studies, such as that of the young man who must decide whether or not to apply for multiple copies of a free CD offer, the solution may appear more obvious. Be careful, however, not to push the "right" answer on students. Also be aware that while the solution may seem apparent to you, it may be much less obvious to your students.

In this course, all the case studies (except for the case "Stop or Not" found on the Resource Page for session 1) are true. We have found from experience that these have a down-to-earth realism that appeals to students far more than fictional cases. After exploring a case, students decide what *should* be done to resolve the dilemma. Once they've decided that, you can tell what *actually* was done to resolve the dilemma, for better or for worse.

Practical Tips

■ Be a good listener. Case studies demand that you do more listening than talking. Try not to be intimated by times of silence. Any discomfort will wear off when students realize you care enough about their responses to give them time to think.

■ Encourage students to think through a case before jumping to a solution. The approaches in this course will help students look at biblical evidence and consequences before they suggest a solution.

■ Wait until students have thoroughly discussed a case before revealing how the case actually turned out and before giving your own opinion. If and when you do offer your opinion, present it as an option you believe is in keeping with God's Word, not as the only right answer to the dilemma.

■ Ask questions that encourage thought. When a student says, "I think that so-and-so should have done this or that," ask, "Why do you say that?" or, "What Bible passage or principle supports that view?" or, "Good, but what would be the consequences of her doing that?" If a student gives an answer that is flat-out wrong, direct him or her back to the case.

■ Use a variety of approaches when discussing cases, as this leader guide suggests throughout. At times you'll want to lead the class through a case, explore various options with them, list supporting rationale, and arrive at a recommended solution. Other times, you'll want to have students work in small groups, as is often advocated by this leader's guide. Small groups may act as a jury in one case, perform a role play in another, or look at biblical principles and project consequences in yet another. Working in small groups often helps build student involvement and promotes freedom of expression. If you're teaching a really small class—say, three or four students— you'll need to find ways to work around procedures that require several groups of two to four students each. Often this leader's guide will give you ways to adapt a group procedure to a small class.

■ Point students toward the truth. As the mature Christian in your classroom, you need to hold up the standards of Christian ethics by which we judge our decisions and actions. In other words, you need to point students toward the truth, to teach them that some answers to moral issues are clearly more Christian than other answers.

Writing Your Own Case Studies

From time to time you may find yourself thinking, "I know a case that would really work great for this commandment." We say, "Great—write it up!"

Writing your own cases takes time, of course, but it's not all that difficult.

Keep your eyes open for case study material in newspapers and magazines. If you stick to the facts and quotations presented in the articles, formal permission to write a case study just for your class (not for publication) should not be required. Of course, if you write a case based on someone else's unpublished experiences, permission to use the case with your class is both necessary and ethical.

Here are a few tips for writing case studies.

- In the first paragraph, state the problem and indicate the need for a decision. In the next couple of paragraphs, give the setting and introduce the characters. Next, narrate past events, including dialogue (quotations, conversations) as much as possible. In the final paragraph, restate the focus and call for a decision.

- Generally, use the past tense and third person. Avoid injecting your opinion by your choice of words. Be as objective as possible.

- Conceal the identity of persons and places involved, except for well-known cases. When inventing new names for places or persons, don't try to be funny or cute. Maintain the reality of the case by using ordinary names.

- Allow room for debate about what the decision-maker should do.

Your students may also enjoy writing their own cases. To facilitate that process, you may want to allow fictional cases rather than insist the cases be true.

the way we decide

SESSION FOCUS

The way we decide to act in a given situation is influenced by the moral principles (basic ethical assumptions) we hold.

SCRIPTURE

Luke 6:43-45

SESSION GOALS

- to give examples of tough decisions faced by teens

- to give examples of principles that influence people's decisions and behavior

- to show how these principles influence the way we behave in a specific situation

- to think about why we decide and act as we do

SESSION AT A GLANCE

Learning Activity	Materials	Time
1. *Small Groups: "Don't Know What to Do!"* Small groups list examples of "tough decisions" faced by their age group.	Newsprint, markers	10-15 minutes
2. *Bible Study: Good Tree, Bad Tree.* We discuss Luke 6:43-45, with its image of a tree and its fruit, to pinpoint the link between our beliefs and our actions.	Bibles, notecards, pens	5-10 minutes
3. *Case Study: Stop or Not?* We read a case study, then look at how twelve principles (or moral values) could affect our actions in a specific situation that requires us to make a tough decision.	Pens, Resource Page: "Case Study: Stop or Not?" (one copy per student, p. 123)	20-25 minutes
4. *Closing: Guidance from God's Word.* We find and read a verse or two from passages that guide or comfort us when we're faced with problems or tough choices (alternate activity for students not familiar with the Bible is a responsive reading of selected passages).	Bibles	5-10 minutes

SESSION BACKGROUND

This is a course in Christian ethics. More precisely, it's a course in *how* to make Christian moral decisions.

In this course, you'll be teaching your students to see the complex moral issues that underlie quite ordinary acts. You'll be pointing out the compass points of concern—for God and neighbor, for family and self, for justice and mercy—between which swings the needle of their decision-making. You'll be teaching them how to make moral choices according to Christian ethical principles in concrete life situations. You'll be helping them to form for themselves a Christian pattern of moral living.

This first session helps your students see that the decisions we repeatedly (and often unthinkingly) make in specific situations really spring from moral principles. This holds true even if our pattern of decision-making is impulsive and unconscious instead of reasoned and deliberate. What I do and what I believe are linked together, although that link is often not as clear and tight as it should be.

The Bible uses the image of a tree to illustrate this link between beliefs and actions. "No good tree bears bad fruit, nor does a bad tree bear good fruit" (Luke 6:43). Ethics draws from the well of faith the standards and principles that give the water of life to moral behavior. Our own particular moral pattern, our accustomed way of acting and reacting, is largely formed by the principles we have drawn from our faith and our faith community.

Say I stop and help a woman who has stumbled and fallen. So does John Smith. Our actions are the same. Together we help her up, each supporting one arm. Together we pick up the scattered packages. We're both courteous and kind. Yet the *why* of our actions, the reason for our decisions, the principle behind our kindness may be quite different. I may help because my self-image requires it; John may act out of loving concern. I may feel superior in serving; John may feel humble in helping. I may assist a woman who falls but never a man; John may as readily help either. I may hesitate for fear of legal complications; John may never consider such a thing. I may remember how my mother fell and no one helped her; John may remember the Good Samaritan.

In some cases differing moral principles cause different decisions; in other cases, for differing reasons, people do the same thing. But in either case the moral dimension is prominent. This session means to help your students see that the moral character of an action comes partly from the act itself (some acts—like stealing, slander, or sexual abuse—are intrinsically bad) and partly from the ethical motives, goals, and principles that the act embodies. Such insight is a necessary first step to moral reflection and Christian decisions.

This session points your students toward the unique character of Christian ethics and poses a question: In contrast to other patterns of moral decision-making, what makes ours Christian? If our faith is truer, our hopes higher, and our love deeper than that of other religions, does that make our morality, our daily living of that faith, better? If Confucian Chinese have the Golden Rule, devout Muslims meticulously obey the law, and animistic Inuit share the last crumb of food with hungry strangers, how are we better?

The answer to this key question comes in the next session and is actually the theme of the entire course. For what you will be teaching is not a better ethical or moral strategy, but how we, who are Christ's, must be Christlike "in all our living."

—Harvey A. Smit

LEADING THE SESSION

**1 Small Groups:
"Don't Know What to Do!"**
Materials: newsprint, markers

Divide into groups of two to four students each. Give each group a marker and sheet of newsprint. Tell them they have five minutes to list and briefly describe as many tough decisions as they can—decisions they or others have had to make or might have to make that could lead them to think, "I really don't know what to do!"

If groups need help in getting started, here are a few suggestions to pass along:

- issues with parents
- friendship issues—choosing friends, clashes with friends over the rightness or wrongness of some activity
- peer pressure
- personal stuff—tough decisions you've made or might have to make in the not-so-distant future.

After five minutes, have someone from each group display the group's sheet and present the group's examples of tough decisions. There's no need to discuss the examples—just get them out there. You may want to note examples that more than one group mentioned.

Point to a couple of the more challenging decisions (on the newsprint sheets) and ask: **Suppose you had to make this decision—how would you know what to do, what to decide?** Welcome all suggestions but do not discuss details at this point. Instead, explain that this course—*No Easy Answers*—will look at this very question and give us practical help and guidelines in making decisions like these, and many more.

TIP
Don't be concerned if some groups come up with silly examples, such as that huge decision about what kind of toppings to put on the pizza. The point is just to let kids list the decisions they see as difficult and challenging. It's OK if some are just for fun or less challenging than others.

TIP
Save the newsprint sheets of tough decisions kids listed. You may be able to use them later in the course, perhaps as starting points for the group to write their own case study.

---

activity adaptations

If this is an opening session with a new class, consider asking kids to introduce themselves by giving an example of a tough choice they've recently made—or a choice they might have to make soon. Examples could be serious or funny. Afterward, ask how they will decide what to do in these (or other) situations.

Or have each group invent and dramatize one tough decision someone their age must make—a situation in which he or she is not sure what to do.

TIP

Of course you don't have to do the notecard thing— you could just ask kids to say what they think the passage means. But writing out the verse and what it means is worth the extra time it takes because it gets everyone (not just the talkers) involved and encourages a more thoughtful response.

2 Bible Study: Good Tree, Bad Tree

Materials: Bibles, notecards, pens

Distribute Bibles and notecards, and ask someone to read Luke 6:43-45. Have everyone copy verse 43 on the notecard: "No good tree bears bad fruit, nor does a bad tree bear good fruit." Then say something like this: **Suppose you wanted to explain to a friend— in plain English—what Jesus is saying here. What would you say?** Have students write their response under the verse they just copied.

Invite each person to read aloud what he or she wrote. Emphasize the idea that what we are on the inside determines what we are like on the outside—the way we talk, the way we act. What's in our heart shapes what comes out of our mouths and what we do with our hands. Ask, **What does this have to do with making decisions and choices?**

Listen to comments (there may not be any!) then summarize by saying something like this: **Our decisions and actions are influenced by what's in our heart, by the values and principles we have about life. In a minute, we're going to see how this works in a specific situation.**

3 Case Study: Stop or Not?

Materials: pens, Resource Page: "Case Study: Stop or Not?" (one copy per student, p. 123)

TIP

Go around the circle for this activity, asking each person to read a principle aloud and to give an initial response.

Distribute a photocopy of the resource page to each student. Read the case aloud to the class. You may want to mention that while this is a fictional case, the remaining cases used in the course actually happened.

Work through the list of principles with the class. For each principle, ask students to respond to the question on the handout: *If I held this principle, would I stop or drive on? Why?* Be flexible as you listen to responses. Remember that any one moral principle could motivate different responses—see examples below.

1. *Glandular principle:* Drive on! Who wants to get soaked? Why ruin my good clothes!

2. *Me-first principle:* Why stop? Won't do me a bit of good. Besides, the whole thing could be a setup for robbery. If someone is in that car, he'll have to take care of himself. I've got more important things to do right now. Maybe I'll call the cops later, if I get a chance.

3. *Universal principle:* I hate to go out there, but it's the logical thing to do. Suppose no one in the world ever bothered to help someone in trouble? What a lousy world this would be! I'll help.

4. *Golden Rule principle:* Sure, I'll stop. It's the least I'd want someone to do for me.

5. *Conscience principle:* I'd feel awfully guilty if I didn't stop. Something tells me it's the right thing to do.

6. *Pass-the-buck principle:* Look, I've got to get to graduation. Other cars will come along. Let someone else help. I wouldn't know what to do anyway.

7. *Good Samaritan principle:* Someone could be injured in that car. If there is, I have an obligation to help. I'll take a look and see what I can do.

8. *Legal principle:* If I stop, I'd have to park partly on the highway and that's against the law. Too bad . . . better just go on. *Note:* this principle doesn't fit our case very well; we mention it because it is a key principle for discussing the rest of the cases in this course!

9. *Minimum risk principle:* I'll call the cops when I get to school. No sense taking any chances.

10. *Tradition principle:* Helping people in trouble is what our family always does. I'll stop.

11. *Sanctity of life principle:* Someone's life could be in danger here. That life is more important than my inconvenience.

12. *WWJD:* It's pretty obvious what Jesus would do in this situation. Since he is my example, I better stop.

After reviewing the list, discuss the questions in the handout.

- **Do you have any other principles to add to this list—motives or attitudes that would help determine what we should do?** Students may mention Christian love as a guiding principle set forth by Jesus himself. Other possibilities: putting God and others before self, giving unselfishly, serving others, and so on.

- **Give an example of how one moral principle could motivate different responses.** If students need help on this one, give them an example and let them supply others. For instance, the "me-first" principle might motivate me to drive on because I'm unwilling to take the risk or trouble of stopping; on the other hand, if I have a great urge to see my name in print or my face on TV, that same principle could influence me to stop and help. Similarly, the conscience principle could influence me to stop and help, but if my conscience is callused, I'd probably drive right on by. Even the Good Samaritan principle may not, in these times of increasing crime and litigation, make me stop. It may only direct me to the nearest phone to call the police.

- **Do our moral principles influence the way we decide and act (a) a little (b) some (c) a lot (d) not at all? Why?** We hope, of course, that kids say "a lot," since that's the key idea of this session and course! Whatever they say, it's a good idea to give your group a chance to react, now that they've seen how principles can affect actions in a specific case. So use this opportunity to listen to your students. Some may feel that most of our decisions are made on the spot, without much conscious thought or moral reasoning. You may want to point out that moral principles often function at almost a subconscious level, but we still base our actions on them.

- **What do you think you might do if you were actually in that situation—stop, drive on, or something else? Why would you do it? What principle would influence you? (You may use a principle that's not on the list, if you wish.)** Give students time to think this over, then invite responses. Because they are familiar with the parable, some students may mention the Good Samaritan principle. If they do, use this opportunity to point out that Christian principles are derived from the Word of God. Ask students if they remember the question the parable addressed (Who is my neighbor?). Also ask how the parable might help us if we were actually faced with the decision of stopping or driving on (by reminding us that all people are our neighbors and therefore deserving of our help and love).

Other Christian principles students might mention include: sanctity of life, the Golden Rule, love for others, conscience, and WWJD. Obeying the law, while not very applicable in this case, is also a key factor in Christian decision-making. Next week's session will focus on the principle of love within the law of God. The remainder of the course follows the Ten Commandments.

activity adaptation

Instead of just reviewing the twelve principles with your class, ask them to pair off and have each pair role-play how one or two principles would determine whether they would stop or drive on. One of the two role players should be the person in the ditched car, the other the driver of the car passing by. The latter sees the car in the ditch, does his moral reasoning out loud, then either stops or drives on. Let the kids have fun doing this—piteous cries for help from the ditch, driver rolling down the window peering out into the rain, maybe looking at his watch or hunting for an umbrella, and so on.

option: apply the principles

If you have extra time, have students work in small groups and apply the twelve principles to one or more of the situations they listed at the beginning of today's session.

4 **Closing:
Guidance from God's Word**
Materials: Bibles

Remind students that the decisions and actions of everyday life ought not to be separated from the Word of God and prayer.

If your students are familiar with the Bible, ask them to find and read a verse or two from a passage that gives them guidance or comforts them when faced with problems or tough choices.

If your students are not familiar with the Bible, invite them to turn to Psalm 139 (or a passage of your choosing). Divide into two groups and read verses 1-14 responsively as your closing prayer.

option: alternate closing

Or close today's session by returning to step 1 and the tough choices that students listed. Have each student pick one tough decision, then pray aloud for God's help and for wisdom, should they ever have to make that decision.

the *ought* of love

SESSION FOCUS

The heart of Christian ethics is love. Love seeks the good of others within the law of God.

SCRIPTURE

Matthew 22:37-40; John 14:15; Romans 13:8-10; 1 John 5:3

SESSION GOALS

■ to explain why love alone or law alone isn't enough

■ to describe the scriptural relationship between love and law

■ to be more sensitive to the demands of Christian love on our own decisions and actions

SESSION AT A GLANCE

Learning Activity	Materials	Time
1. *The Greatest of These: The Love Principle.* Small groups work to select one biblical principle that should influence our actions and decisions more than any other. We read Scripture passages that support the idea that love is this key biblical principle.	Bibles (study Bibles with a concordance in the back will be helpful), newsprint, markers	10-15 minutes
2. *Situations: Love Alone.* We look for the common idea in five situations, all of which demonstrate that "love alone" isn't a good guide to moral behavior.	Pens, Resource Page: "The *Ought* of Love" (one copy per student, p. 125)	10 minutes
3. *Situations: Law Alone.* We again look for the common idea in five other situations, all of which demonstrate that "law alone" isn't a good guide to moral behavior.	Pens, Resource Page: "The *Ought* of Love"	10 minutes
4. *Love and Law: Making the Connection.* We look up Bible passages that mention love in the context of law. We write statements that connect love and law the way the Bible does.	Bibles, pens, Resource Page: "The *Ought* of Love"	5-10 minutes
5. *Law: It's Not What You Think.* We discuss our attitude toward the law, then describe how living by the principle of "love within law" could change our attitude or actions toward someone during the week ahead. We conclude by praying for each other.	Pens, Resource Page: "The *Ought* of Love"	10 minutes

SESSION BACKGROUND

In this second session, you will be teaching the heart of Christian morality—ethical love. This love, which Christ commanded, is a love for God and neighbor; it is unquestionable, the final and absolute standard of all our conduct. "Love," says Romans 13:10, "does no wrong to its neighbor. Therefore love is the fulfillment of the law."

When we say *ethics,* we tend to think *norm.* When we say *doing right,* we're inclined to think *obeying law.* That's not wrong. Obeying God's commands, doing what's right and good according to God's directing Word, is an indisputably essential element of proper Christian living. God's norms show the believer what ought to be done. But as one Christian ethicist has remarked, "Norms are absolutely necessary but not necessarily absolute." Love is the absolute. Three things abide: faith, hope, and love, "but the greatest of these is love" (1 Cor. 13:13).

Still, to say only this might be very misleading. Like most young people, your students probably like the idea of love. It's free, personal, spontaneous. And it fits with the individualistic "if it feels good, do it" guide to right acting. Equally, they may dislike the idea of law. It's binding, impersonal, regimenting. That's often *their* idea of love and law. So Christian morality as love alone, love unlimited, love unruled attracts them.

Old people tend to be more cautious. Life has bruised and matured them. Through life's painful pricks and high hurdles, they've learned the value of limits and the utility of law. They've lost the boundless optimism of youth and gained the restrained balance of age. The free and unexpected are no longer so welcome. Law frames a stable society and supplies a secure setting. Lawlessness is frightening anarchy. To most older people, a passing police officer is a token of peace, not a threat to freedom.

Within that context of differing generational views, and in contrast to our culture's odd split of private love and public justice, you must teach that the love that guides our living, the love of Christ realized in us, is neither lawless love or loveless law. It's love in principle, love that seeks the good of others within and through God's law. This is the *ought* of love. This is the love of which our Lord was speaking when he said, "If you love me, you will obey what I command" (John 14:15).

In the Bible, love and law, mercy and justice, are never opposites. To love God and neighbor is the heart of the law. To rightly meet the law's demands one must act in love. The two are intertwined and interspersed. They fit together. Love, in the Bible's terms, is not a fluctuating feeling, not our modern appreciative response to another's beauty, intelligence, or athletic skill. Love is undeserved, unreserved reaching out in concern to a fellow human being. Love seeks the other's concrete good in acts of mercy and justice. Love doesn't follow the easy way of indulging the young and pleasing the old. It seeks the good that may be unpleasant for both, but is truly for their good. In all this, love reflects the God who is love but is also holy, righteous, and just in every way.

So love knows and seeks its neighbor's good. Exactly what that good is isn't left to our opinion. God's law tells us what is good. God shows us the good we must lovingly perform (Mic.6:8). And love fulfills (completes) the law. Love internalizes the law, draws it in and makes it part of itself, freely following its guidelines.

If love is the force that moves the needle and directs the way, law is the compass point that gives the bearings. Together, as obedient love, they steer us to our proper course.

The *ought* of love is no verbal gimmick, no clever combination of opposites in a mere word solution. Rather it reflects the word of Christ: "My command is this: Love each other as I have loved you" (John 15:12).

—HAS

LEADING THE SESSION

1 The Greatest of These: The Love Principle
Materials: Bibles (study Bibles with a concordance in the back will be helpful), newsprint, markers

When all are present, remind the group of last week's list of principles that affect our decisions and actions. Ask students to recall a few of these principles (glandular, me-first, universal, and so on.)

After your brief review, divide into groups of two or three. Give each group a sheet of newsprint, a marker, and a Bible. Say something like this: **What biblical principle do you think should influence our decisions and actions more than any other principle? Jot down your idea on the newsprint. Also, please add at least one Bible passage that supports your idea. Use your Bibles to help you do this. You have five minutes.**

After five minutes, check to see if most groups are finished. Someone from each group can present their group's idea, using the sheet of newsprint. It's very possible that all groups will select love as the key biblical principle but some may argue for other ideas, such as obedience (law), justice, fellowship, kingdom, covenant, the person of Christ, the Holy Spirit, worship, and so on.

Express appreciation for all ideas, and then focus on love as an often-cited key to Christian ethics, or our actions and decisions. If you haven't already read Scripture to support this view, have volunteers read such passages as Matthew 22:37-40, John 15:12, and 1 Corinthians 13:13, as well as other passages the students may suggest.

Explain that our session today will help us understand what "love" means when we make tough choices and decisions.

TIP
Spend more time reviewing if several students showed up today who were absent last week. Have someone describe the case study "Stop or Not?" and have others give examples of how the different principles could affect one's action in that case.

TIP
This activity calls for some Bible knowledge, so try to place students unfamiliar with the Bible with those who are more familiar (see Activity Adaptation below if most of your students aren't very well acquainted with Scripture). If students have study Bibles available, encourage them to look up a key word in their principle in the concordance at the back of their Bibles. This may lead them to key passages that support their principle.

activity adaptation

If most of your students are new to the Bible, or if you want to save time for other parts of the session, modify step 1 by simply asking the entire class what principle they think most Christians would cite as *the* key, guiding principle behind their actions and decisions. Receive their ideas with appreciation, then focus on the principle of love, having students look up the passages mentioned in the regular step on page 21.

2 Situations: Love Alone
Materials: pens, Resource Page: "The Ought *of Love" (one copy per student, p. 125)*

Distribute copies of the resource page to each student. Have someone read through the five situations under "Love." Give students a few minutes to write out the common ideas they find in the statements.

activity adaptation

Steps 2 and 3 can be done in small groups of two to four students each. Have half of the groups work on the statements about "love," and the other half work on the statements about "law." Give the groups ten minutes to complete their work, listing the common ideas on their handouts. Then have the groups present their findings, first reading aloud the five situations, then identifying the common ideas they found among the five situations. Guide the discussion as necessary, using the suggestions found in steps 2 and 3.

Or have the groups role-play the five situations. This increases involvement and interest but, of course, takes more time.

When students are ready, review their responses. Expect (and welcome) some variety. Samples:

■ All the statements suggest that love often has good intentions or motives. All the people involved mean well.

■ All the statements suggest that this kind of love could have bad consequences (you may want to explore a few of these).

■ All the statements suggest a defective love that seems to be missing something.

These concepts are all valid, and perhaps your students will find others as well. But the concept we'd like students to discover for themselves is a little more complicated. Briefly stated, it is *love without law*. If you can't steer students to this concept, you may end up telling them (but be careful not to imply that this is the *only* idea the statements have in common.) Once the concept has been discovered, take a few minutes to have students show how it is demonstrated in the statements. Here's a quick guide:

1. Love allows a couple to set aside God's law about chastity.

2. Love for neighbor and enemy blinds a victim to justice.

3. Protective love for a friend permits ignoring the eighth commandment.

4. Love as a *feeling* substitutes for love as *obedience.*

5. Love allows a teacher to set aside—for no apparent good reason—his own rule that all other students had to follow.

A good test of understanding this concept is to ask students to invent their own illustrations that fit the pattern. Maybe you'll have time for that in your class today.

Conclude by saying something like this: **Are we all agreed, then, that love alone isn't enough, that love without law or obedience really isn't love at all?**

3 Situations: Law Alone
Materials: pens, Resource Page: "The Ought *of Love"*

TIP
Since you've summarized with a question, look for affirmation before moving on. If students still aren't sure, be patient and try to clarify as best you can.

Point out that a second ingredient in Christian ethics—our actions and decisions—is law. By "law" we mean obedience to God's Word (not just the Ten Commandments, though they are the heart of the law). Explain that all the situations in the next section of the handout illustrate some ideas about law. Repeat the procedure you followed in step 2.

If love by itself isn't enough, neither is pure legalism. That's the idea we'd like to focus on in this section (as before, receive with appreciation other ideas about law the five statements have in common). Students will probably agree that the law alone is not the proper basis for Christian ethics. There may be times when

■ a lie is necessary (statement 1).

■ healing work must be done on the Sabbath (statement 2).

■ murderers deserve a second chance (statement 3).

■ the church needs to forgive and restore (statement 4).

■ a student has a compelling reason not to hand in a paper on time (statement 5).

Again, if you have time, ask students to supply their own illustration of the concept.

Conclude by summarizing along these lines: **So, are we agreed that if love alone isn't enough, neither is law alone enough? That somehow the two have to be put together?** As before, look for affirmation before moving on.

4 Love and Law: Making the Connection
Materials: Bibles, pens, Resource Page: "The Ought *of Love"*

Having seen that neither love alone nor law alone is the key Christian moral principle, students should be ready to understand that the two belong together, that they are intertwined.

Ask for volunteers to read aloud the three Bible passages mentioned in the handout. The passages all mention love in the context of law.

■ John 14:15—Love means obedience, says Jesus.

■ Romans 13:8-10—Love is the fulfillment of the law. Eugene Peterson's paraphrase *The Message* spells this out in more ordinary language: "When you love others, you complete what the law has been after all along."

■ 1 John 5:3: Love for God means obeying God's commandments.

After reading the passages, give students time to respond to the two questions in the handout:

■ **What do you think the *ought* of love refers to?** A good answer is that it refers to obeying God's law. This "ought" is necessary because we live in a sinful world.

■ **Try to write (in one sentence) what these passages teach us about the relationship between love and law.** A good answer would be to simply reiterate what any of the three passages (above) say. A handy three-word summary is "Love within law." A more complete summary is "Christian love is seeking the good of others within the law of God."

You may want to ask students to copy one of these statements or one like it next to their own in the handout.

5 Law: It's Not What You Think
Materials: pens, Resource Page: "The Ought *of Love"*

Admit to your class that when you stack the two ideas—love and law—next to each other, most people lean heavily toward love. Ask questions like these:

■ **Do you agree that "love" is generally a more appealing idea than "law?" If so, why do people often feel negatively about God's law?**

■ **In your own day-to-day experience, does God's law help you in any way? If so, how?**

The main thing here is to listen your students. It's likely that some will say that God's law steers us away from doing what's wrong; for example, it warns us not to use God's name lightly in our conversation, not to dishonor our parents, not to lie or cheat or hurt our neighbors. It serves as kind of a guide to moral living.

TIP

If students take a negative attitude toward the law, you may want to comment along the lines suggested by Rev. Jack Roeda. **It's a mistake to suppose that God gave us laws to keep us from enjoying life. We can be sure that God is delighted to see us happy. After all, God made this world in such a way that the very necessities of life— eating, drinking, sleeping, reproducing—are positively delightful. No, God's purpose in giving us the law is for our good.**

If students don't bring it up, mention these "do nots" represent the bare minimum requirements of love. It's important that we also apply the commandments in a positive way, as Jesus does in his Sermon on the Mount. To love our neighbors, therefore, not only means that we are forbidden to kill them. Read Answer 107 (from the Heidelberg Catechism), as printed on the bottom of today's resource page:

God tells us
> **to love our neighbors as ourselves.**
> **to be patient, peace-loving, gentle,**
> **merciful, and friendly to them,**
> **to protect them from harm as much as we can,**
> **and to do good even to our enemies.**

Refer students to the final heading in the handout ("Living Your Love.") Read the directions aloud: **Think of one specific way this idea of loving others—within the bounds of the law of God—could affect your attitude or actions toward someone in the coming week. Be practical—think of something you would actually be willing to do. Jot your response below.**

Invite students to share what they wrote with two or three other students. Then close the session by having students pray for each other in the small groups.

---

option: alternate closing

Instead of the discussion about law (above), you could shift the focus to the principle of love. Give students some quiet time to think about someone they know (or have read about) who really exemplifies Christian love, as we have been discussing it today. Tell them the person could be well-known (such as Mother Teresa) or someone close to home (such as a friend or relative, teacher or employer). Then ask for volunteers to tell the rest of the class about the person they've chosen and to describe his or her act(s) of Christian love (students need not mention names if they would rather not). Close the session by asking students to offer prayers of thanks for the person they mentioned.

the first commandment

SESSION FOCUS

We are to worship God alone and love God above all, shunning whatever "idols" we may be tempted to worship instead of God.

SCRIPTURE

Mark 10:17-22

SESSION GOALS

- to restate the first commandment as a message from God to our world today

- to insert contemporary examples of idolatry into the story of the rich young man (Mark 10:17-22)

- to recognize how a contemporary case study ("Sitting at the Altar") relates to the first commandment and to suggest a possible "love within law" solution to that case

- to identify something in our lives that we may idolize and to be the recipient of prayers from the group that ask for help in facing down those idols

SESSION AT A GLANCE

Learning Activity	Materials	Time
1. *No Other Gods: Billboards.* Small groups rewrite the first commandment as if they were writing a "message from God" billboard for a modern audience. We also look at several quotes from catechisms and elsewhere that can deepen our understanding of the commandment.	Newsprint, markers, masking tape, Resource Page: "First Commandment" (one copy per student, p. 127)	10-15 minutes
2. *Bible Study: "Go, sell . . ."* Students use a reader's theater format to present the story of the rich young man (Mark 10:17-22), then work in pairs to improvise a dialogue between Jesus and a contemporary young person who wants to know what he or she should abandon or put in its rightful place in order to follow Jesus.	Bibles	10-15 minutes

3. *Case Study: Sitting at the Altar.* Small groups discuss this case, identify "love alone" and "law alone" responses, and finally suggest a response that meets the "love within law" principle discussed last week. (Alternate case and discussion approach provided.)	Case Study Card: "Sitting at the Altar" (or alternate: "Meet You at the Mall"), newsprint and makers, instructions written out for small groups	20-25 minutes
4. *Personal Idols: Prayers for the Battle.* Students think of something they are tempted to idolize, then participate in a "focus prayer."	no materials needed	5 minutes

SESSION BACKGROUND

With this session you begin to focus on ethical principles—the basic, biblical imperatives that direct our moral choosing and doing. The guide for this study will be the Ten Commandments.

Some find the Ten Commandments too old, too flavored with prohibitions. Others think they are too general, not specifically Christian enough. As someone has observed, the Ten Commandments sketch the minimum conditions necessary for the survival and welfare of any society, not the maximum demands of Christian love. In a course on ethics, why not use Christ's clear commands to his New Testament followers in the Sermon on the Mount, or Paul's specific description in Ephesians 5 and 6 of what it means for us to "walk in love" as "imitators of God"?

But the Reformed tradition does not permit that sort of ethical contrast between Old and New Testaments. Rather, the ten words have been the ancient jars into which the wine of the new ethical instruction is poured, the framework to which the brick and mortar of the new spiritual commands are attached. This follows the pattern Christ himself established in the first part of his great sermon (Matt. 5).

The covenant law of Exodus 20, an abiding expression of God's will for us, becomes a useful and uniquely comprehensive catalog of basic ethical principles when seen in the light of Christ's fulfillment and obeyed in the freedom of the Spirit. The Heidelberg Catechism makes it the pattern for our life of gratitude, the vehicle for expressing our thanks to God for salvation in Christ.

This section focuses on the first commandment. It does so first through the story of the rich young man in Mark 10 and then through your choice of two case studies. The story from Mark shows that serving Christ alone, placing him first, and following Christ have profound implications for our lifestyle—for the moral pattern of the use of this world's goods that characterizes our way of living.

The love and worship of our God are the great and first commandment. This has clear priority. Obedience to it sets the tone for all moral compliance. It maps the loyal path and sets our feet on its commencement. In all our moral decision-making, pleasing God comes first.

As God's chosen people, we are called to acknowledge, trust, love, fear, and honor God alone. We may have no other gods—whether they be the god of high technology that keeps us glued to a computer screen (first case study) or the god of materialism that lures us to the mall (alternate case study). To honor and serve these—and other—gods endangers our salvation and is nothing less than idolatry.

Idolatry—the word slides by our ears. Who worships idols today? "The heathen in his blindness bows down to wood and stone"—to quote the hymn that quotes Kipling. Your students can easily join Isaiah (ch. 44) or Jeremiah (ch. 10) as they jeer at these primitive gods, fashioned with axes, fastened with nails, decked with silver and gold. Idols—gods that cannot see or know or speak.

I wonder what those two prophets would say of the TV sets and computer screens before which we sit in fascinated adoration. These idols speak—and tell us all the wrong things. They teach us concern only for how we smell, how we dress, and what others think of us.

Luther said, "Whatever your heart clings to and confides in, that is your god." What holds our heart captive, what we value most, what fills our deepest need is our god, our idol. That is our treasure. "For where your treasure is, there will your heart be also" (Matt. 6:21).

If your students admit (as they are given a chance to in the last part of today's session) that they too have other gods, you will have accomplished much today. That's the first step toward awakening a desire to live only for the one true God.

—HAS

LEADING THE SESSION

1 No Other Gods: Billboards

Materials: newsprint, markers, masking tape, Resource Page: "First Commandment" (one copy per student, p. 127)

Begin today's session by explaining briefly that we will be following the structure of the Ten Commandments for the remainder of the course, taking one commandment and one case study related to that commandment each session.

Distribute Bibles and ask someone to read the first commandment (Ex. 20:1-3). Break into groups of two to four students each and distribute a sheet of paper and markers to each group. Give instructions along these lines:

Not too long ago a series of billboards, all signed "God," featured a variety of intriguing messages addressed to folks driving their cars down the freeway. For example, one said, *Come to my house before the big game on Sunday.* Another, *What part of "Thou Shalt Not" didn't you understand?* Still another, *I really meant that thing about loving your neighbor.* Working with others in your group, write a billboard message from God that is based on or restates the first commandment that we just read. When you're done, tape it to the wall.

Give groups five minutes to write their billboards. Then display them for everyone to read (leave them on display, if possible, for the entire course).

For a change of pace, have everyone create their billboards on a long roll of tablecloth paper that you've unfurled. The result will resemble an actual billboard and can be displayed on the walls of your room.

Commend all responses, then distribute copies of the resource page "First Commandment" (p. 127). Have students take turns reading whatever you find helpful from this page. You'll find brief quotes from the Heidelberg Catechism, the Westminster Shorter Catechism, and several other sources.

2 Bible Study: "Go, Sell . . ."
Materials: Bibles

Have everyone turn to a Mark 10:17-22. Appoint one student to read the part of the rich young man, another to read the part of Jesus, and another to read the opening and closing narration in verses 17 and 22. After the reading, ask what the young man's idol was (his great wealth and possessions) and how much this idol meant to him (too much).

Ask students to work with one other person to improvise a dialogue between Jesus and a contemporary person their age. What things or idols might Jesus tell us we should put in their rightful place if we want to be his disciples? In other words, what do we love so much that we are reluctant to give it up to obey and serve God? Give the pairs a couple of minutes to plan, then have them present their dialogues to the rest of the class.

activity adaptation

To save time (or simply to avoid too much work in small groups), you can ask the class as a whole to suggest things (idols) that we should abandon or put in their rightful place if we want to be Jesus' disciples. Make a list on newsprint of the items suggested by the class. Save the list for use in the last step of the session.

3 Case Study: Sitting at the Altar
Materials: Case Study Card: "Sitting at the Altar" (or alternate: "Meet You at the Mall"), newsprint and makers, instructions written out for small groups

Distribute copies (from student resources envelope) of either of the two case studies for this commandment. Explain that this case, and all cases used in the remainder of this course, actually happened (names and some details have been changed to protect the identity of those involved). That's important for your students to know because they will respond with much more interest to something that really happened than to a fictional case. Also tell your class that real cases were chosen because they provide real-life lessons. As part of our learning, we ought to keep telling ourselves, "This really happened! This person agonized, lost sleep, wept over this issue." So it's important for us not only to understand but to empathize as well.

Explain that later in today's session you'll tell them what the person making the decision decided to do. Read the case study aloud to the class.

TIP

Each commandment gives you two choices of cases. Our choice is listed as the first case, and it's the one for which we supply a more detailed discussion guide; our second choice is listed as an alternate. However, you should feel free to use the alternate case if you think it would be more appealing to your students or if you find it has a stronger link to the commandment being studied.

Both cases this week get at "idols" common to the age group you're teaching. "Sitting at the Altar" focuses on a mother of young children who worships at the altar of her computer; "Meet You at the Mall" deals with an attraction that one high school counselor describes as a "substitute god" for many students, offering "an inextricable connection between having name-brand clothing at great sacrifice and being in the company of people whose status hangs on clothes. Both urges are joined at the mall." Be careful here, though—in some areas it is particularly the younger students, often in junior high, who are most caught up in the mall thing.

By the way, if you want to extend the number of sessions in this course, an easy way is to take both cases for some of the sessions.

Once again, divide into small groups of three to five students each. Write the following instructions on newsprint or on your board prior to class and display where groups can refer to them throughout this activity:

In your small groups I'd like you to decide these three things:

- **What might be a "love alone" choice for the decision-maker?**
- **What might be a "law alone" choice for the decision-maker?**
- **What do you think is the best "love within law" option for the decision-maker? Why? (Consider the consequences of your choice on all those involved in the case.)**

Tell the groups they have ten minutes to discuss the questions above and to record the group's answers. Make sure each group has a Bible and a sheet of newsprint and a marker for recording their response to the questions above.

Remind the groups not to immediately leap to a solution to the case but to follow the three-part process described above.

TIP
When doing group work, it's often best to choose the groups yourself so that you will have a balance of talkers and non-talkers. If possible, let groups go to an area where they will not be distracted by other groups—in the hall, in a corner of a stairwell, in the church auditorium. And have the group members designate roles for each group member to play. For this group work, have groups designate a leader, a recorder, and a presenter.

Of course, you can lead the class through the questions rather than have them work in small groups, if you think that will promote better discussion. It will take less time but may not involve students as fully as working in small groups.

Before the groups report, ask:

■ **What does this case have to do with the first commandment?** It should be obvious that the computer has become a kind of idol for Linda—it is what she cares about most, more than the kids, more than Gord. Life to her without the computer isn't worth living. She is indeed "sitting at the altar" and is totally devoted to her idol, even dropping out of church to sustain her habit.

Continue by agreeing with all groups on the first two parts of the assignment:

■ A "love only" response from Gord could mean just leaving the situation the way it is, hoping that Linda will eventually get over her addiction to the computer. While this may seem like the tolerant, loving thing to do, especially when combined with Christian counseling, it's not a good choice. It would likely be very harmful to the children, who already lack the attention of their mother; to Gord, who would continue to be frustrated; and to Linda herself, who would almost certainly sink deeper into her addiction, leaving her real needs unaddressed. Such a choice would fail to bring in the element of law that prohibits idolatry, that says parents have a responsibility to their children, and spouses a responsibility to each other. (It might be interesting to ask if the groups think that Gord has already given a "love only" response by buying Linda a second computer).

■ A "law only" response from Gord could mean leaving his wife for good, taking the kids along, and not helping Linda with her addiction. While Gord could be within his legal rights doing this—she's had an affair of sorts with her cyberlover and has proven to be a negligent wife and mother—such a decision would leave the children without any mother whatsoever and would abandon Linda to her addiction. It would not have that element of Christian love that demands we love others as ourselves, that forgives wrong, that seeks to restore and heal.

With these two extremes out of the way, focus on what could be a "love within law" (or love *and*) choice for Gord to make.

■ A love with law (or love *and* law) approach starts by recognizing that Linda is seriously addicted. Her past history and actions, her ongoing inability to stop, her neglect of the children and Gord all point to an addiction that needs outside help to be broken. Given that, a "love and law" response could begin with (a) disconnecting the Internet and (b) insisting that Linda get intensive addiction treatment because she is too sick to get better by herself. Gord needs to insist that Linda fulfill her responsibilities as a mother and that, once she recovers, she must participate in a addiction recovery group and avoid all contact with the Internet. And he needs to pledge Linda all his support during and after this time of intensive treatment.

If she refuses treatment, Gord needs to make it clear that he intends to separate from her, keeping the children with him, until she chooses to seek help for her addiction.

In addition, however, Gord himself needs to take all the steps he needs to stop being codependent and to become a real help to her. He needs to seriously place God back at the center of their marriage, their family, and his own personal life. He needs to take more responsibility at home as a husband and father by spending more time with Linda and the kids. By participating in counseling, he needs to help Linda attempt to get at the real cause of her addiction (boredom? lack of people to talk to? frustration with the kids?). Perhaps a daytime job, either paid or as a volunteer, with daycare for the children could be part of the solution.

After thorough discussion of the case, you may tell the group how it was resolved. Gord did not take the computer away; instead, he continued to plead with his wife to care more for the kids. The grandparents, knowing the situation, stepped up their attention to the kids. Linda remains addicted to the computer.

option: alternate case study: meet you at the mall

For this case, we suggest you ask small groups (or the whole class) to answer questions like these:

- **What does this case have to do with the first commandment? In what way can meeting a bunch of kids to go shopping and hang out at a mall be an idol or substitute god?**

- **What, if any, are the reasons Taryn should go to the dinner and skip the mall?**

- **What, if any, are the reasons she should skip the dinner and go to the mall?**

- **What do you think she should do? Why?**

In your discussion of this last question, ask students if they can think of other commandments (besides the first) that might be involved in Taryn's decision. Would honoring parents and grandparents (fourth commandment) be a factor here? How about truth-telling, keeping one's word to friends (ninth commandment)? In general, the harder the decision, the stronger the clash between "competing" commandments or moral priorities. In Taryn's case, the basic commandment—"no other gods before me"—outweighs the others, if she is indeed guilty of making the mall an object of her devotion and love, the way her father alleges. In addition, honoring parents/grandparents, in this case at least, may carry more weight than a kind of "promise" to friends to go with them to the mall.

After your discussion, you can tell your class that Taryn wrote her grandparents a note and went to the mall with her friends, not only that Friday night but many others thereafter.

TIP

Listening carefully to your students' responses will give you some good clues as to how to handle future case studies in this course. It may take some time and effort to teach your students to think through a case instead of immediately jumping to a solution. See the Introduction to this leader's guide for some suggestions on how to accomplish this.

4 Personal Idols: Prayers for the Battle

Materials: none needed

Remind the class of the first commandment, pointing to the "billboards" they made in step 1 as quick summaries of its meaning. Also remind them of the "idols" they inserted into the story of the rich young man (step 2). Then ask each person to think of something that they personally are tempted to idolize, something that may threaten to be a kind of god to them, that commands their time and commitment and devotion. Be sure they understand they will not have to share this information.

Explain that we will end our session with a "focus prayer," in which you (leader) will say a name of one student at a time. After each name, the rest of the class will focus on that student, silently asking God to help him or her fight the battle against his or her personal idol, whatever it may be. If you wish, ask students to lay their hands on the shoulders of the person they are praying for. Allow about fifteen seconds or so of silence, before mentioning another name.

the second commandment

SESSION FOCUS

God is holy and should be worshiped in no other way than what God has commanded in Scripture.

SCRIPTURE

Exodus 20:4-6; Psalm 95:6; Isaiah 40:18-25; Matthew 16:16; John 4:23-24; Romans 10:17; 1 Corinthians 1:23; 2 Peter 1:19

SESSION GOALS

- to relate the second commandment to how God wants us to worship
- to list some biblical guidelines or principles for true worship
- to apply these principles to a case study about worship
- to ask God to help us improve our worship in one specific way

SESSION AT A GLANCE

Learning Activity	Materials	Time
1. *Remembering and Worshiping: In the Presence of a Holy God.* We recall times when we felt a strong sense of genuinely worshiping a holy God. We hear the second commandment and a passage from Isaiah describing God's holiness, then observe a time of silence.	Resource Page: "Second Commandment" (one copy per student, p. 129)	10-15 minutes
2. *Bible Study: Worship—the Way It's Supposed to Be.* We draw on our own experiences and a variety of Scripture passages to list qualities that define true, God-pleasing worship.	Resource Page: "Second Commandment," newsprint, markers, masking tape	15-20 minutes
3. *Case Study: Sweating It Out.* Small groups discuss this case, keeping in mind the principles of true worship from the Bible study, and suggesting reasons why the person involved should or should not participate in a sweat lodge religious ceremony. (Alternate case and discussion approach provided.)	Case Study Card: "Sweating It Out" (or alternate: "Wicca in the Woods"), newsprint and markers, paper slips for ballots	15-20 minutes
4. *Resolution and Prayer: Improving Our Worship.* We commit to improving our worship in one specific way, then pray with a partner for God's blessing on our commitment.	Notecards, pens	5 minutes

SESSION BACKGROUND

Last week we looked at the first commandment, with its emphasis on *who* we worship: only the one, true God. Making gods out of computers or shopping malls is idolatry. Today we focus on the second commandment, with its emphasis on *how* we ought to worship this one, true God.

Keeping the *who* and *how* distinction in mind will help you see why we assigned these case studies to the second commandment. Both center on how we are to worship God. The first case basically asks if a Christian may participate in a "sweat lodge" religious ceremony; the alternate case asks how tolerant Christians ought to be of the "Wicca" movement. How we worship is clearly involved in both cases.

The second commandment forbids the making and worshiping of idols or images of the one, true God (Ex. 20:4-7). Why? What's the harm in images as an aid to worship?

We can give human reasons. Our likenesses always take away from God. They subtract, never add. They hinder, never aid. Our human tendency to portray the One we are worshiping often prevents our truly worshiping the One who will not be portrayed by people.

But here is the real point: the Lord our God is a jealous God—jealous not of competitors (for there is no other God) but of God's own image. God's holiness must be guarded. Our images, visible or mental, always contain some element of error. Without our intending it, they disfigure God.

So where God's image and worship are concerned, God leaves nothing to human devising. The tabernacle in the Old Testament was designed and laid out by God alone. And when Jesus Christ was born, everything was kept under God's direct control. Angels gave precise messages. Nothing was left to human decision—not even the place of Jesus' birth and residence. In Jesus Christ, God carved and drew for us the true image of himself in his Word. "The Son is the radiance of God's glory and the exact representation of his being" (Heb. 1:3).

God reserves the right to portray himself among people. God reminds us how a holy God is to be worshiped and remembered. For us, this is forbidden territory. We are to worship God, as the Heidelberg Catechism says, "in no other way than what God has commanded in his Word."

And how is that? Your students will be given a chance to answer that very question in the Bible study part of today's session. They will likely give a broad range of good, acceptable answers. We suggest you focus on several key areas indicated by the passages on the resource page.

- First, we need to worship with total sincerity of heart, "in spirit and in truth" (John 4:23-24).

- Second, we need to worship in full recognition of the holiness of our awesome God: "To whom will you compare me? Or who is my equal?" says the Holy One (Isa. 40:25).

- Third, we need to approach this holy God through Jesus Christ, our mediator, "the way and the truth and the life," the only path to the heart of God (John 14:6).

■ Fourth, we need to pay close attention to the Word of God, through which God instructs us and equips us for righteous living (2 Pet. 1:19).

Applying these and other general criteria to worship won't necessarily lead to quick and easy answers about what does—and what does not—constitute worship that is pleasing to a holy God. But these are the basics, the *oughts* of worship, the signs that point us in the right direction as we talk about—and participate in—the worship of the one, true God.

—HAS

LEADING THE SESSION

1 **Remembering and Worshiping:
In the Presence of a Holy God**
Materials: Resource Page: "Second Commandment" (one copy per student, p. 129)

When students arrive, ask each to think of a time when he or she felt a strong sense of genuinely worshiping a holy God, whether in church, in nature, during a retreat or youth convention, on a service project, or wherever. As students reflect on this, you may want to share your own example of a time when you felt you were truly worshiping God.

Go around the circle and ask students to share their thoughts, giving them the option of saying "pass" if they wish.

If students have a hard time thinking of a specific instance, ask them to think of worship settings that help them worship God.

> ## activity adaptation
>
> If your class is large, you may want to have students share in small groups of three or four students each. You need not ask for any kind of "reporting" from the groups when they're finished.

After the time of sharing, distribute copies of the resource page (p. 129). Ask someone to read the second commandment. Comment that the difference between the first commandment ("no other gods before me") and the second commandment is that the first focuses on *who* the one, true God is, and the second focuses on *how* that God is to be worshiped. You may also want to read the brief line from the Heidelberg Catechism that reinforces the "worship" theme of the second commandment.

Conclude by inviting your students to worship with you. Ask a good reader to read aloud Isaiah 40:18-25 from the resource page. Then ask students to simply observe a moment of silence, to allow themselves to come into the presence of a holy God. If you think your students can handle it, you may want to invite them to kneel before God, should they wish to do so.

Instead of step 1 of the regular session, have students work in small groups to make lists of things they would judge to be intolerable or even just wrong in a worship service (examples: praying to other gods, bringing in statues of saints as aids to worship, worshiping with indifference or apathy, worshiping without sincerity, worshiping without reference to Jesus or to the Bible, worship that's boring, and so on). Review their lists, then bridge to the second commandment and its emphasis on proper worship as "God has commanded in his Word."

2 Bible Study: Worship—the Way It's Supposed to Be

Materials: Resource Page: "Second Commandment," newsprint, markers, masking tape

Refer again to the resource page and note the box that says:

What does God look for when we worship? In other words, how can we worship in a way that pleases God? Draw on your own experiences and the passages and other material on this page. Jot your ideas here.

Let students work in groups of two or three. Ask the members of each group to take turns reading the passages aloud, pausing after each to jot down (on a sheet of newsprint and on their resource page) what they think it says about worship. They should also draw on their own experiences in worship to make their lists. Allow no more than ten minutes for the groups to work (see tips for working in small groups in session 3).

When the groups are done working, have them tape their lists to the wall or otherwise display them. Review the lists together. It's likely that students will come up with many ideas that we did not intend them to find in the passages! That's great. But do call attention to these four key ideas:

■ We need to worship with total sincerity of heart, "in spirit and in truth" (John 4:23-24).

■ We need to worship in full recognition of the holiness of our awesome God (Isa. 40:18-25; Psalm 95:6).

■ We need to approach this holy God through Jesus Christ (John 14:6).

■ We need to pay close attention to the Word of God (2 Pet. 1:19).

Ask the groups to refer to the lists on the board as we talk about a case that involves the way we worship.

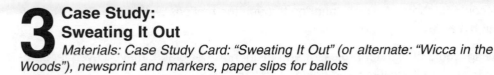

3 Case Study: Sweating It Out

Materials: Case Study Card: "Sweating It Out" (or alternate: "Wicca in the Woods"), newsprint and markers, paper slips for ballots

Distribute copies (from student resources envelope) of either of the two case studies for this commandment. The directions that follow assume you're using the main case study, "Sweating It Out." If you choose the alternate case ("Wicca in the Woods"), please see the option on page 40.

Read the case aloud to the class, then ask how it relates to the second commandment. Help the class frame the key question as they look at this case study: **Was the sweat lodge ceremony an example of worship that was pleasing to God and that a Christian could therefore participate in? Or was it something else?** Ask the class to keep that question in mind as they discuss the case.

Divide into two groups. Ask one group to list (on newsprint) all the reasons they can think of why Marisa should stay and participate in the worship ceremony. Ask the second group to list all the reasons they can think of that she should leave. Tell group members you want them to be objective here, to list reasons even if they feel Marisa should take the opposite action.

---

activity adaptation

You really don't want more than five or six students in a group. If you have a large class, divide into four rather than two groups. Have two groups work on reasons to stay and two groups work on reasons to leave.

Give groups no more than ten minutes to work. Then review their lists. Some sample responses follow.

Reasons Marisa should stay:

- Her friend's pastor saw no problem with attending (though he based his advice on the incorrect assumption that it was going to be more of a cultural history presentation than a religious ceremony).

- Marisa's professor, something of an authority on this topic, said the prayers that were offered were to a Creator-God who was the same as the Christian God.

- Marisa's friend, who was a Christian, stayed; likely there were other Christians who stayed and participated.

- The ceremony seemed to respect the holiness of God (shoes removed, respectful prayer) and the worshipers were obviously sincere.

- Leaving would seriously offend the hosts. Was it right to interrupt a religious ceremony like this, even if she disagreed with it?

- Marisa was uneasy but wasn't entirely sure that the ceremony was offensive.

- She could be there physically and "go through the motions" without really participating in her heart.

- Leaving would offend her professor and might hurt her grade, maybe even jeopardize her passing the course and getting certified.

- We simply don't have enough facts to know if the ceremony was acceptable to Christians or not (debatable, but could well be cited as a reason to stay).

TIP

You may want to explain that our conscience is not some mysterious inner moral sense, but that it is tied to what we have learned from God's Word and from the Holy Spirit working in our hearts. Of course, our conscience has been corrupted by sin, and its possible that our conscience can become hardened or oversensitive. But it still clearly calls us to do the right and avoid the wrong. When our conscience speaks, we must always listen. As John Calvin said, "Whenever we take a step in opposition to conscience, we are on the high road to ruin" (commentary on 1 Cor. 8:11).

Reasons to leave:

- From the facts that are available in the case, this seems like a questionable worship service. The chief elder who led the service invoked multiple spirits to enter the room and prayed to the "gods" of water, air, earth, and fire (sounds like an appeal to multiple gods, though the instructor said otherwise). The case says nothing about Christ being mentioned or Scripture being read, both key in Christian worship. And the worship seems more self-centered than God-centered, a human ritual of cleansing more than anything else.

- Marisa's professor was wrong in forcing students to attend.

- Marisa's conscience was tugging at her, telling her to leave from practically the moment she arrived.

- The principle of being faithful to one's conviction is more important than offending the host or endangering one's standing with a professor.

When you feel the facts on both sides of the case have been reasonably aired, distribute small slips of paper and ask the students to write "stay" or "go" or "not sure" on the paper. Collect the slips, including your own, and announce the results.

Tell the class that Marisa did not leave, though she wished throughout the ceremony that she had not come. She refused to take off her shoes, prayed to God silently when others invited the spirits into the lodge, and did not participate in the confession ceremony. She admitted she thought her grade would have been affected negatively if she did not attend the ceremony.

option: alternate case study: wicca in the woods

Wicca is a cult that's growing in popularity, especially among young people who are attracted to the latitude and freedom given by the Wiccan rede or rule: "If it harm none, do what you will." Because Wicca (meaning simply "craft" or "witchcraft") is central to this case study, we suggest you spend some time first talking about it, especially in light of the Bible study on worship you just completed.

Ask your students: **Does Wicca—as described in the case study—promote the kind of worship a Christian can participate in?** Have your students look at the statements that describe Wicca as they answer this question.

Because Wicca is a decentralized religion with a very loose system of beliefs, some might think that a person could be a Christian and a Wiccan at the same time. That is definitely not true, as the case study illustrates. Note the following facts about Wicca with your students.

- The Wiccan view of God is seriously flawed. Wiccans may be polytheists, worshiping many gods and goddesses, or monotheists, worshiping one god with two distinct halves, male and female. Pantheism is also admired. This is clearly counter to the Christian notion of "one true God."

- Wiccans do not accept the Trinity or the deity of Christ.

- Wicca is permeated by the idea of magic (its members are all called "witches"). Magic, says Andrew Kuyvenhoven, is "the old craft of manipulating a supernatural power for one's own benefit." This can lead to all sorts of curious rites and rituals. (In fairness to Wiccans, we should note that sacrificing animals—a practice common to Satanism—is shunned.)

- Most Wiccans believe that nature is sacred—some go so far as to worship earth as the Great Mother Goddess.

- Though Wiccans often gather in covens, each coven is autonomous and its members can pretty much believe and practice what they please, as long as their practice remains within the general Wiccan rede or rule. Individual Wiccans are free to interpret their faith as they wish. This is contrary to the Christian faith, with its emphasis on holding mutually-accepted beliefs and teachings and worshiping in community with other believers.

- Many Wiccans believe in a form of reincarnation (this fact is not mentioned in the case study).

With this preliminary discussion out of the way, ask students what they think Shelly's parents should do. Have them suggest some options that they think would be a good "love and law" response. What would they do if they were Shelly's parents? If you have time, encourage students to role-play a meeting between Shelly and her parents, implementing their ideas for a good solution to the case in the role play.

Given Wicca's numerous violations of what constitutes true Christian worship, any good "law" response should warn Shelly of the dangers of Wicca and insist that she drop all association with it. The poster and other Wicca stuff gets tossed! At the same time, Shelly's parents should express their love for their daughter and urge her to stay at home. Given her history of running away and her problems with drugs and chastity, Shelly's parents should also insist on professional counseling of some kind.

How did this case come out? You can tell your students that before Jake and Pam could reach a decision, Shelly took matters into her own hands and left with her boyfriend. She quit school, as she threatened to do. She had a baby with her boyfriend, and then married an older guy. Her parents do not know if she's still involved with Wicca.

TIP
To the best of our knowledge, the information about Wicca presented in the case study is accurate and reliable. If you want more information about Wicca, you can check out any of dozens of Wicca websites, most run by self-proclaimed Wiccans or Wiccan groups (see, for example, www.wicca.com and www.wicca.org, or simply search "Wicca" on your network browser).

4 Resolution and Prayer: Improving Our Worship
Materials: notecards, pens

Distribute notecards and ask each person to think of one way he or she could improve the way he or she worships God. Explain that it doesn't matter where this worship takes place—in church, at school, at home in private devotions, at youth group, or wherever. Have them write their thoughts and resolve to implement their idea during the coming week. The cards can be taken home as reminders.

Invite students to find a partner, share their thoughts, and pray aloud for each other. If you wish, begin next week's session by having partners share what they did to implement their idea for improving their worship.

option: alternate ending

You could choose to end today's session as you began it—by focusing once more on God's holiness. Have students find and read short passages of Scripture that help them sense God's greatness and holiness. Or, if you prefer, read Psalm 136 responsively. Then use a circle prayer format to invite students to finish this phrase with their own words of praise or thanksgiving or petition: "O, God, because you are holy, I . . ." (bow down before you; worship and adore you; ask that you make me holy . . .).

the third commandment

SESSION FOCUS

The third commandment requires us to honor God's name, not only by our words but also by our actions.

SCRIPTURE

Exodus 3:15; 20:7; Psalm 115:1; Acts 4: 12; Philippians 2:9-11; Colossians 3:17; James 3:9-10

SESSION GOALS

- ■ to explain why God's name is holy and must be honored
- ■ to give examples of how we misuse God's name by what we do as well as by what we say
- ■ to apply the third commandment to a case study about misusing God's name
- ■ to ask God to help us honor God's name in a place where we feel challenged to do so

SESSION AT A GLANCE

Learning Activity	Materials	Time
1. *Name Game: People We Respect.* We play a guessing game involving names of people we respect. Then we read about God's name from the third commandment.	Small slips of paper, fine-tipped markers or pens, old hat, duct tape	15 minutes
2. *Bible Study: Name Above All Names.* We read a litany of biblical and confessional material related to the third commandment, then discuss how we misuse God's name and why God's name must be revered.	Resource Page: "Third Commandment" (one copy per student, p. 131)	10 minutes
3. *Case Study: On the Praise Team.* Small groups discuss the case study, projecting consequences of various choices and applying the third commandment and other biblical principles to the case. (Alternate case and discussion approach provided.)	Case Study Card: "On the Praise Team" (or alternate: "The Cussing Canoeist"), Bibles	20-30 minutes
4. *Prayer: Honoring the Name.* We draw a picture of a place where we feel challenged to honor God's name. We write and offer short prayers asking God to help us honor God's name in that place.	Notecards, pens	5 minutes

SESSION BACKGROUND

When your students hear the third commandment—"Do not misuse the name of the LORD your God"—most will think immediately that the command forbids them to misuse God's name by swearing or cursing. They're right, of course. And we need to hear this command increasingly in a culture that too often uses the name of God only as an expletive. Even persons raised in Christian families and communities hear plenty of profanity on television, at the movies, in recorded music, at ball games, at school functions, and elsewhere. They may not use such language themselves, but hearing it does not trouble them all that much. To persons raised in more exposed surroundings, profanity used for emphasis is a normal part of language.

In either case, using or tolerating profanity doesn't seem to provoke much guilt—ironically, since this is the only commandment that mentions guilt.

Even though we may feel guiltless, we are all guilty of breaking all of the commandments. We confess that doing so is our natural tendency. Today's session should increase your students' awareness of how our words and actions may violate this third commandment.

This commandment came to Israel at a time when using a god's name was considered a means of using the god's power. Incantations, curses, and sorcery used names of gods to hurt enemies (remember the story of Balaam in Numbers 22-24). Israel was forbidden to use God's name in this way. The one God, who would be worshiped alone, who would not be imaged in any way, would also not permit the name to be used for merely human purposes. It must not be used sacrilegiously, but only for worship and praise.

You'll find this aspect of verbal abuse of God's name in the alternate case study, "The Cussing Canoeist," a case that made the national news a few years back. Our main case—"On the Praise Team"—deals with a much broader interpretation of the commandment, that we can misuse God's name not only with our words but also with our actions.

Taking God's name in vain goes far beyond using an occasional "God damn" or "Jesus Christ" in conversation. It extends to all misuse, disrespect, and neglect of God's holy name. Our listless, half-minded prayers, hymns sung while yawning, sniggering jokes, and casual talk about the "man upstairs" are examples of such abuse. It includes those times when our actions in church or in other "religious" settings do not match our actions at school or on the street.

Why is dishonoring the name of God so serious? Unlike Old Testament believers, we do not usually suppose a name represents a person's essence. Neither do we believe that naming a name gives us magical powers. For us, names are just symbols, handy ways to designate people and things so we can talk about them.

Still, our own name is somehow precious to us. We can't avoid the persistent feeling that it's somehow part of us and we're part of it. Our name involves our dignity. If it is dishonored, so are we. Even the children's rhyme "Sticks and stones may break my bones, but names will never hurt me" is often a sort of counter-incantation. Misuse of our names *does* hurt us, sometimes more than a swung stick or thrown stone.

If that's true for us, it's even truer for God, whose name was and is a capsule form of holy revelation, a sign of God's divine presence. God's name is the core of God's revelation. God explains: "This is my name forever, the name by which I am to be remembered from generation to generation" (Ex. 3:15). Jesus is the name of God revealed for our salvation (Acts 4:12), and one day every knee shall bow at the sound of that name (Phil. 2:9-12). Jesus came into the world to manifest God's name (John 17:6). The church's task on earth is to proclaim that name and not deny it (Rev. 3:8). God's name is the knowledge of God in this world.

In the revelation of God's name to us humans, we have been entrusted with God's dignity. For our salvation, God's holiness has been exposed to us, in spite of God's knowledge that we will misuse and blaspheme God's name. God's holy name has been put in our mouths and on our tongues.

Our task is to hallow that holy name. By blessing, praising, and sincerely worshiping God in our words and by our actions, we are to display proper reverence and awe. We are to proclaim God's name to all peoples. We are to make holy what is most holy in this our unholy world—the name of God.

—HAS

LEADING THE SESSION

**1 Name Game:
People We Respect**
Materials: small slips of paper, fine-tipped markers or pens, old hat, duct tape

Here's a fun "name game" that will help you bridge into the third commandment and the respect it requires us to have for God's name.

Begin by distributing two slips of paper and a marker or pen to everyone. Give instructions like these: **On each slip of paper, please write—in large letters—the name of someone you admire and respect. Don't let others see the names you list. Don't pick a family member or relative or someone only you would know. You may pick someone from your school or church or community, or a national or international figure.**

After a minute or two, collect the slips and mix them up. Divide the group into two teams. Have someone from team 1 step forward and draw one of the names without looking at it. Take the name, tape it to an old hat, and have the name-bearer face the rest of the class so they can read the name. Team 1 is to give clues to the name-bearer that will help him or her guess the name. They have thirty seconds to do this. If the name-bearer guesses correctly, his team gets one point. Repeat the process with someone from team 2, and continue until all the slips of paper are used up.

TIP
If you ended last week's session by having partners share how they would attempt to improve their worship this week, you may want to take a couple of extra minutes to have the partners meet and tell each other what they did.

---

activity adaptation

To make the game a little more challenging, have the name-bearer ask yes/no questions that the entire group answers. Allow a minute or more per name.

As time permits, pick out two or three names and ask the persons who listed them to tell what it is they admire about the person or why they respect him or her.

Bridge to today's topic by reading the third commandment from your Bible: "You shall not misuse the name of the LORD your God, for the LORD will not hold anyone guiltless who misuses his name" (Ex. 20:7). Comment that God's name—far more than the name of any people we've named in our game—is one that deserves our utmost respect and honor and praise, and that God feels very strongly about that! How strongly? The third commandment is the only one that mentions that God "will not hold us guiltless" if we dishonor God's name.

2 Bible Study: Name Above All Names
Materials: Resource Page: "Third Commandment" (one copy per student, p. 131)

Distribute copies of the resource page (p. 131). Read through the litany (no need to read the location of Scripture passages and confessional material listed in italics). Then discuss with questions like these:

- **What's the first thing that comes to mind when you hear "Don't misuse the name of God"?**

- **On a scale of 1-10—with 1 being very little and 10 being very much—how great is your exposure to profanity (cursing, swearing, taking God's name in vain)?**

- **The third commandment talks about misusing God's name. What are some other ways—besides profanity—that we misuse and dishonor God's name?** See the Session Background for examples.

- **Why is God so concerned about the way we treat God's name? Why is it so important to honor God's name?** See the session background for helpful comments on this key question. The central thing to get across is that God's name represents who God is. God's name is holy, and that holy name is a sign of God's presence. You may want to refer to some of the Bible passages from the litany that get at this idea.

3 Case Study: On the Praise Team
Materials: Case Study Card: "On the Praise Team" (or alternate: "The Cussing Canoeist"), Bibles

Distribute copies (from student resources envelope) of the case study for this commandment. The directions that follow assume you're using "On the Praise Team." If you choose the alternate case ("The Cussing Canoeist"), please see the option on page 49.

Read the case aloud to the class, then divide into small groups of three to five students each. If your class is small or if students aren't effective in small groups, simply use the questions to lead a general discussion of the case.

TIP
Side 2 of the resource sheet relates to misusing God's name through profanity. If you're using the alternate case study ("The Cussing Canoeist"), you'll have an opportunity to bring in side 2 material. If you're using the main case study ("On the Praise Team"), you can omit side 2 altogether or bring it into the above discussion, if you wish.

Ask the groups to discuss the following questions. Give the groups about ten minutes for their discussion. Then review their findings with the entire class, using the comments below as a guideline.

- **Who in this case violated the third commandment? How?** Hannah misused God's name not only by her profanity but also by her double standard of behaving piously in church settings but immorally in other settings. An interesting question to discuss is whether Katie too might be violating the third commandment by her silence.

- **What are some possible consequences (to Katie, to Hannah, to the congregation) if Katie confronts Hannah with what she saw?**

  Katie: Given Hannah's character, it's likely that Katie could be met with outright denial and rejection ("It wasn't me you saw—you're dreaming!"). Hannah could tell Katie that even if it were true, it was none of Katie's business—butt out! It's possible, of course, that Hannah would eventually come around to admitting the truth, and even change her ways. But Katie would take a huge personal risk in confronting Hannah. On the other hand, she at least would have the satisfaction of acting on her conviction, of doing what she thought was right.

  Hannah: If she denies Katie's claim, then she sinks deeper into a network of lies and more lies, and possibly some pretty intense struggles with her conscience. It would get harder and harder for her to lead the praise team, knowing there were people out there who realized she wasn't sincere. If she accepted Katie's claim, she could be on her way to change for the better. But she might feel she would have to give up her singing on the praise team until she made the necessary changes in her life.

  The congregation: It faces the very real possibility of Hannah resigning from the praise team, at least for a time, if she faces up to her guilt and attempts to change. On the other hand, a sincere Hannah leading in worship has got to be better than an insincere Hannah!

- **What are some possible consequences (to Katie, to Hannah, to the congregation) if Katie remains silent and does nothing?**

  Katie: Silence for Katie would be a "no risk" response, but it would likely mean a continuing struggle with her conscience. Nor would her worship experience likely improve as long as Hannah remained on the praise team.

  Hannah: Silence would likely mean no change in the status quo for Hannah, unless someone else besides Katie confronted her. It would mean the continuation of a lifestyle that was not pleasing to God.

  The congregation: Silence would likely mean no change in the status quo.

- **What biblical principles—besides the third commandment—might help Katie decide what to do?** Respect and reverence for the name of God is at the heart of this case (see earlier comments).

  Hannah is doing something that Katie thinks violates that commandment—all the while pretending to be a super Christian, even leading God's people in worship. Katie

TIP
Because of the complexity of projecting consequences, you may want to suggest that groups need not write their findings on newsprint this time. However, groups should appoint someone to take notes and to make a presentation to the class. Groups should also appoint a leader.

TIP
Your students may object to Katie's confronting Hannah because she could have made a mistake—it might not have been Hannah dancing on the table. It was dark, and how could she be sure? The case takes pains to point out that Katie was very sure of who and what she saw; however, if you have future trial lawyers in your class who insist she could have been mistaken, grant them the point and ask that, for the purposes of this case, they assume Katie saw Hannah, as she said she did.

can act to start a process that might end that misuse of God's name—and restore a fellow believer to her Lord.

Katie might also recall that love for others—within the law of God—is the key to Christian decision-making. And that kind of "tough love" can require correcting a friend or classmate, if necessary and if done kindly (see, for example, Matt. 18:16: "If your brother sins against you, go and show him his fault, just between the two of you. If he listens to you, you will have won your brother over").

Katie needs to be sure that her motive in confronting Hannah is to help her see her sin and change her ways. Merely desiring an improved personal worship experience is probably too selfish a reason to confront Hannah; however, if Katie feels that God is being dishonored by Hannah's presence on the worship team, that might be a more legitimate reason to confront her.

■ **All things considered, what would you advise Katie to do? (You may suggest alternate options in addition to remaining silent or confronting, if you wish.)**

Here are some questions that may surface:

—Is Katie close enough to Hannah to confront her on this?

—Does Katie have any right to act on information she gained covertly, during a kind of "spying" episode?

—Is Katie sure that Hannah's misbehavior is chronic, or was the incident an isolated one?

—What are Katie's motives in confronting Hannah?

—Is the overall impact of confronting likely to be positive or negative?

Listen to what your students suggest, then tell them how the case came out. Katie did describe what she saw to her father, months after the summer experience. She did not talk to Hannah but still feels she should have. It is hard for Katie to worship with Hannah still leading the praise team.

option: extension of case study

How do you go about lovingly confronting a friend about behavior you consider dead wrong? It's not easy, any way you look at it. So how might it work? Ask for two female volunteers to role-play a confrontation between Katie and Hannah. Let the rest of the class critique the role play, reacting to what was said and how it was said, and offering constructive suggestions.

4 **Prayer:**
Honoring the Name
Materials: notecards, pens

Invite each person to think of one place (home, school, church, work, locker room, and so on) where they are most challenged to honor God's holy name. Give them a notecard and ask them to draw a picture of that place on the card. On the flip side of the card, invite them to write a one- or two-sentence prayer, asking God to help them honor God in that place this week.

Students may pray their prayer aloud or silently, as they wish. Encourage them to bring the cards home and place them where they will see them every day.

option: alternate closing

Psalm 99 pays beautiful tribute to the awesome, holy name of God. Ask for a volunteer to read it aloud, or read it responsively with the class.

Remind your students that Scripture says someday every knee shall bow to Jesus Christ and every tongue confess his name. Invite students to kneel with you, if they wish, as you say a prayer along these lines (pausing to give students time to offer their own petitions):

> Holy God, I confess that I have misused your holy name. Please forgive me for . . . (pause)
> I bow before you and your son, Jesus Christ, in complete reverence and awe. I especially praise you for . . . (pause)
> Help all of us to acknowledge and praise your name in everything we do. In the name of Jesus, Amen.

the fourth commandment

SESSION FOCUS

The fourth commandment requires that we set aside a day for worship, for rest, for doing what's good for ourselves and for others.

SCRIPTURE

Exodus 20:8; Leviticus 3:3; Matthew 28:1; Luke 4:16; Mark 2:23-27; 3:1-5; Hebrews 10:24-25

SESSION GOALS

- to describe how and why the Old Testament Sabbath changed to the New Testament Sunday (Lord's Day)

- to cite biblical guidelines for observing the Lord's Day

- to apply the fourth commandment to a case study about keeping the Lord's Day

- to offer prayers focusing on our use of the Lord's Day

SESSION AT A GLANCE

Learning Activity	Materials	Time
1. *Sunday Survey: What's OK, What's Not.* We line up along a continuum to indicate whether we think certain Sunday activities are OK or not OK.	Bible, tape, two signs: *OK, Not OK*	10-15 minutes
2. *Bible Study: The Road from Sabbath to Sunday.* We complete a Bible study of how the Sabbath changed to the Sunday, and what the Bible says we need to do to please God on "the Lord's Day."	Bibles, pens, Resource Page: "Fourth Commandment" (one copy per student, p. 133)	10-15 minutes
3. *Case Study: Sunday at the Store.* Small groups discuss this case study, applying the fourth commandment and other biblical principles to the case. (Alternate case and discussion approach provided.)	Case Study Card: "Sunday at the Store?" (or alternate: "Big Game, Big Choice"), newsprint sheet with questions for small groups	20-25 minutes
4. *Closing: Written and Spoken Prayers.* We complete sentence starters about the Lord's Day, then pray aloud.	Notecards, pens	5 minutes

SESSION BACKGROUND

The fourth commandment tells us to keep one day in seven as the Lord's Day. Of course, this doesn't mean the other six are free to use as we wish. Rather, it gives a moral imperative that all our times must serve God and all our days be holy to the Lord. Still, as a means to that end, "a certain definite day is set aside for worship and so much rest as is needful for worship and hallowed meditation" (*Acts of Synod,* 1881). This official position was first taken in the Christian Reformed Church in 1881 and has parallels in most other Reformed denominations.

So we are to sanctify this day, worship God in it, and use it for our own and for our neighbor's good. It is to be, as our Lord said, a day made for people—a day to do good, not harm; a day to save life, not destroy it (Mark 2:27; Luke 6:9). It is to be a good and holy day.

Be careful to speak of Sunday or the Lord's Day, not the Sabbath. The Sabbath was (and is, for Jews) the last day of the week. It was the day of creation rest. Sunday is the day of Christ's resurrection, the first day, the day of re-creation's beginnings.

For Israel, the Sabbath was a holy day, a day of joy, a day dedicated to the Lord our God (Lev. 19:2-3). This was a day in which work was forbidden so that people, beasts, and (on the seventh year, the Year of Jubilee) the land might rest (Lev. 25:2). Israel kept the Sabbath not with gloom but with gladness.

For Israel, the Sabbath also sounded a note of freedom. It gave escape from the drudgery of daily duties. But further, it released people from burdensome social systems. The fourth commandment in Deuteronomy 5 speaks of Israel's liberation from slavery in Egypt and requires, explicitly, "that your manservant and maidservant may rest, as you do." What an astonishing innovation—giving slaves a day of rest was unheard of! Less precious than beasts of burden, slaves were often worked to death. But on the Sabbath in Israel, slaves also rested. On this day, slave was peer with master.

On both of these features, Jesus clashed violently with the Pharisees. Where they made it a taboo day, he insisted it was a day to *joyfully* serve God by doing good. When they bound people to innumerable Sabbath rules, Jesus taught that this day was made for people (Mark 2:27). The Son of man is Lord of the Sabbath. In it, he sets people *free*.

After Christ arose, Christians gradually began to worship on the first day of the week. Why? Because that day marked the resurrection of their Lord and the beginning of new life. Like the original Sabbath for Old Testament Israel, Sunday for New Testament Christians was a day of victorious celebration and freedom, a day of freedom from weekly routines but also a holy day.

Between Sabbath and Sunday remains a tie of God-ward direction, holiness, joyful celebration, and unique freedom. But there is also a decided shift, exemplified by Christ's contentions with the Pharisees over this holy day. For us Christians there should be no possibility of a legalistically conceived, gloomy taboo day. Christ has renewed it, restored its original moral meaning, and made it the day of victory. It has become the day of new life, the day in which we worship the risen Lord and assert his rule over the entire week.

The main case study for this session ("Sunday at the Store") revolves around the issue of working on Sunday, an increasingly common occurrence for many Christian teens. If nothing else, the case will help them understand the biblical principles and the practical consequences that are involved in deciding to take a Sunday job. The alternate case ("Big Game, Big Choice") revolves around the clash between a teen who wants the freedom to play a championship game with her team on Sunday versus parents who argue that "God doesn't change the rules." On one level, it's a classic Sabbath/Sunday confrontation, though the issue of obedience to parents also plays a role in this case.

The Heidelberg Catechism teaches that Sunday is not a day of taboos but a festive day of rest. It is a day of joy, a day of freedom from weekly routines. But it is also a holy day, a day in which we joy in worshiping with fellow believers and a day that we use for our own and our neighbor's good.

These are the non-negotiables to keep in mind as you discuss just what it means—and does not mean—to keep the fourth commandment today.

—HAS

LEADING THE SESSION

1 Sunday Survey:
What's OK, What's Not
Materials: Bible, tape, two signs: OK, Not OK

Prior to class, tape your two signs (*OK* and *Not OK*) at opposite ends of one side of your classroom. Begin today's session by asking someone to read the fourth commandment from Exodus 20:8-11. Explain that you'll be reading a list of various activities. Each student should find his or her place along the continuum between the signs to indicate to what extent he or she thinks that activity is OK or not OK to do on Sunday. Point out that standing in the middle indicates a "not sure" stance.

Here's a list of statements to read. Pause after each to allow students to take their positions, but do not ask students to give reasons for their position.

1. going to church

2. doing homework

3. watching pro football on TV

4. going to a stadium to watch pro football

5. playing an organized sport with your team on Sunday

6. going to the movies

7. eating at MacDonald's

8. working at MacDonald's

9. painting a house with your youth group

10. shopping at the mall

TIP

Watching where
your students place
themselves along
the continuum will
help you pinpoint
some of the areas of
Sunday observance
that concern them
the most. It will
also alert you to
what you need to
emphasize later in
the session. For
instance, an "any-
thing goes" attitude
would suggest
greater attention to
the holiness of the
day; a legalistic atti-
tude would suggest
emphasis on the
freedom and joy of
Sunday observance.

Invite students to add any other activities on which they'd like to get a reading from the group.

Afterward, ask students to draw some conclusions from this activity. One that's likely to emerge is that Christians differ on what should and should not be done on Sunday. Another might be our tendency to quibble about do's and don'ts instead of realizing what a precious gift of God this day of rest really is intended to be.

option: alternate opening: Sunday customs

Begin by talking about how Sunday observance changes over time. Give an example from your own experience or use these:

- In 1670, two lovers, John Lewis and Sarah Chapman, were arrested for "sitting together and kissing on the Lord's Day under an apple tree."

- George Washington was once arrested for traveling on Sunday.

- As late as 1950, it was officially illegal in Maryland to mow your lawn on Sunday.

Invite class members to give some examples of Sunday customs they've heard their grandparents talk about. Bridge to differing views of Sunday activities that students see around them. Conclude in the same way as the regular step.

2 Bible Study: The Road from Sabbath to Sunday
Materials: Bibles, pens, Resource Page: "Fourth Commandment" (one copy per student, p. 133)

Ask how many agree with this statement: **Sabbath and Sunday mean about the same thing.** How many disagree? How many aren't sure?

Use the results to introduce today's Bible study: "The Road from Sabbath to Sunday." Hand out copies of the resource page and ask someone to read the fourth commandment once more (and, optionally, the excerpt from Q&A 103).

Work through "The Road from Sabbath to Sunday" exercise with the class, asking students to look up Bible passages and fill in the blanks as you proceed. Most answers will be obvious from the fourth commandment itself and from the passages listed in the exercise.

The guidelines from Mark 2:27-28, Mark 3:1-5, and Hebrews 10:24-25 are especially important, since they can be applied to the case study in the next step:

- **Worship with God's people (Heb. 10:25).**

- **Do good toward others (Heb. 10:24 and the example of Jesus in Mark 3:1-5).**

- **Remember that the Lord's Day is a day made for people and that Jesus is Lord of that day.**

Students may have other suggestions to add from their own experiences of attempting to make Sunday a separate, special day. For example, they may feel that refraining from doing the work they ordinarily do during the first six days of the week is a good way to set the Lord's Day apart. Or they may feel that setting aside some "quiet time" on Sunday or some time for recreation is a good idea.

You may want to conclude by reading the second paragraph from the Session Background. It's a good summary of how to observe the Lord's Day.

3 Case Study: Sunday at the Store

Materials: Case Study Card: "Sunday at the Store" (or alternate: "Big Game, Big Choice"), newsprint sheet with questions for small groups

Distribute copies (from student resources envelope) of either of the two case studies for this commandment. The directions that follow assume you're using the main case, "Sunday at the Store." If you choose the alternate case please see the option on page 56.

Working on Sunday is becoming more and more common in the Christian community. Before reading the case study, you might poll your students about their experience with this issue. Has "the Sunday question" surfaced on any job applications they've completed? Have they had to decide whether or not to work on Sunday? If so, how did they feel about having to make that decision?

Read the case study aloud to the class. Then divide into groups of three to five students each (if your class is small or if students aren't effective in small groups, simply use the questions to lead a general discussion of the case). Post the questions below on newsprint where the groups can easily refer to them. Give the groups at least ten minutes to discuss the questions and reach an agreement on what Eric should do. Then review responses with the entire class.

TIP

It's good for students to realize that "biblical principles" don't necessarily hand them easy answers to ethical questions. Sometimes the Bible can seem to offer conflicting advice! As in this case, it takes some careful thought to know how to apply the biblical guidelines to an actual situation.

TIP

You may want to also ask what Eric has done right in arriving at his decision. He consulted another employee about the need for new employees to work on Sunday. He carefully weighed the pros and cons of the issue. He reviewed what he believed the Bible had to say about the matter. He consulted with a trusted Christian (his dad) on what to do. We may also assume that he prayed for guidance. All told, not a bad process to follow!

■ **What biblical principles could help guide Eric's decision?** Notice that Eric indirectly cites the biblical principle of freedom from legalistic Lord's Day observance. He notes that Jesus himself broke the legalistic Sabbath rules of the Pharisees. And he realizes that rules about work that applied to the Sabbath do not necessarily apply to the Lord's Day. Yet this "freedom in Christ" view must be tempered by the clear biblical command to set apart the Lord's Day, to use it for worship and for doing good. At least one thing is clear: if he does work on Sunday, he should also make every effort to find time to worship with God's people.

■ **What reservations does Eric have about taking the job?** Eric prefers to spend his Sundays worshiping with his family and spending time with them. To him, working on Sunday "is a pain." He questions the need for people to shop on Sunday, and he's frustrated that his own Sunday would be sacrificed to the customer's convenience. And he's concerned that working on Sunday might make it become "just another day" to him, a result that would clash with his parents' teaching that Sunday is a time for worship, rest, and family.

■ **If he feels this way, why is he considering taking the job?** Obviously, Eric needs the money to help pay for his college tuition, money he can't probably make anywhere else. If he doesn't take the job, he might end up borrowing so much money that he'll go deeply into debt. His freedom now on the Lord's Day could enslave him to the bank for years to come. In addition, he believes that the Bible does not forbid working on Sunday. And he thinks he can find time to worship after work. Besides, many of his Christian friends work on Sunday too.

■ **What would you advise Eric to do? Why?** Let the groups give their recommendations and briefly summarize their reasons. What do they think Eric actually decided to do? Let them know that he decided to work at the store, though giving up family time and regular worship with his congregation has not been easy for him. He would still prefer to find a job that pays equally well but doesn't require Sunday employment.

option: alternate case study: big game, big choice

Read the case study to the class. Then divide into small groups of three to five students each. If your class is small or if students aren't effective in small groups, simply use the questions to lead a general discussion of the case.

Give the groups fifteen minutes to discuss the four questions on page 57 (have the questions displayed on newsprint for all the groups to see. Afterward, call on various groups to give their responses to the questions. Suggested answers follow the questions.

- **Based on our Bible study of the fourth commandment, who in this case—Rachel or her parents—is closest to interpreting it correctly? Why?** Rachel could argue that she is simply exercising her freedom in Christ to fulfill her obligation to the team. She clearly is not violating the Lord's Day by working; playing the game would be something she would enjoy, something fun and recreational. She might even say that participating is a way of "doing good" on the Lord's Day by showing others she cares about them and the team.

  And she might well fault her parents for not making their stand clear before Rachel even joined the team or went to the semi-final games, which her parents knew might involve playing on Sunday.

  Rachel's parents can point to the importance of worship on the Lord's Day, something we don't know Rachel will or will not be doing (the case doesn't say). They can also argue that the Lord's Day should be a holy day, a separate and special day best celebrated with family, not by participating in organized sports. They can point to the tradition in which they raised Rachel and the importance of sticking to what you believe.

- **What other commandments or biblical principles are involved in this case?** Clearly, the fifth commandment is right up there with the fourth in this case. Rachel's parents have expressed their strong wishes for Rachel not to play. Note, however, that in the end they left the choice up to Rachel. Had they insisted on her return, Rachel would have broken the fifth commandment if she'd decided to play on Sunday. The question now is, Can Rachel play without showing some disrespect of her parents?

  Rachel might argue that the commandment to love others enters in. Her teammates are counting on her, after all. So is her coach.

- **What are the consequences for the persons in this case of (a) Rachel playing ball; (b) Rachel going home with her parents?** If Rachel stays and plays, she might help her team win the game, and she'll certainly win their gratitude and goodwill. Her parents won't have to deal with the anger and disappointment of the other parents and the coach. On the other hand, she runs the risk of disappointing her parents and of feeling guilty about her choice.

  If she goes home, her absence might cause her team to lose the game, and she'll certainly lose the goodwill of the coach and of some of the players and their parents. She'll run the risk of being perceived as self-righteous and inconsiderate of others. On the other hand, going home will certainly please her parents and might even be a positive witness to her teammates about her faith.

■ **What is the group consensus on what Rachel should do?** Listen to what the groups say and the reasons they give for their decision. Be sure to leave room for innovative "solutions" to the problem; for example, Rachel might stay but agree to attend church—perhaps with her parents—before the game, if that's possible. Or she might ask the coach and other parents to talk with her parents about the issue.

So what did Rachel do? Let the group guess, then explain that she chose to go home with her parents on Saturday night, in silent anger. She fought with them on Sunday, cried again, and went back to the tournament site on Sunday night with them after learning that her team had won without her. She pitched in the championship game on Monday, which her team won. When she got back to the team, they were forgiving, as was the coach, but her parents suffered the ostracism of the other parents. Rachel blamed her parents for her decision to go back home with them.

Interestingly, the same issue came up a couple of years later. Rachel was asked to join a state team in basketball to compete nationally, with the likelihood of playing on Sunday. This time Rachel chose on her own not to join. At age seventeen, she is committed to her parents' stance that Sunday is a day for worship, family, and rest from the busyness of her other days.

4 Closing: Written and Spoken Prayers
Materials: notecards, pens

Distribute notecards, one per student. Ask each person to complete one of these two sentence starters:

■ "Lord, help my Sundays to be . . ."

■ "Lord, thank you that Sunday is . . ."

TIP
Be sure to participate in this prayer activity yourself, along with your students.

Allow a minute or two for writing, then invite each person to say his or her prayer aloud. Ask the class to join you in saying (or singing) Psalm 118:24 aloud, after each prayer:

This is the day the LORD has made;
let us rejoice and be glad in it.

---

option: alternate closing

Have students write one way they could make their own celebration of Sunday more meaningful. Invite students to share their written thoughts. Close by saying Psalm 118:24 in unison.

the fifth commandment

SESSION FOCUS

The fifth commandment requires children to honor their parents and others in authority over them.

SCRIPTURE

Exodus 20:12; Proverbs 23:22; Romans 13:1; Ephesians 6:1-4

SESSION GOALS

- to describe what it means to "honor" parents and others in authority

- to apply the fifth commandment and related Bible passages to a case study about honoring a parent

- to honor their parents or other authority figure in a specific way

SESSION AT A GLANCE

Learning Activity	Materials	Time
1. *Role Plays: To Honor or Not to Honor.* We role-play situations that show honor and dishonor to parents or others in authority, then describe what it means to honor them.	Bible, newsprint, markers	15 minutes
2. *Case Study: Please, Won't You Call?* We read today's case, then examine the resource page for supporting arguments on both sides of the issue. Working in small groups, we suggest a resolution to the case and our reasons for it. (Alternate case and discussion approach provided.)	Resource Page: "Fifth Commandment" (one copy per student, p. 135), Case Study Card: "Please, Won't You Call?" (or alternate: "Players Say No to Coach"), newsprint, markers, pens	25-30 minutes
3. *Writing: Letter to Parents or Others in Authority.* We honor parents or others in authority by writing a letter of appreciation to them, then close with a prayer of thanks for those whom God has placed in authority over us.	Writing paper, pens; optional: resource page	10-15 minutes

SESSION BACKGROUND

With this session we begin the law's second table. The first four commandments taught us our proper relation to God and what that requires in daily living. Now comes our proper relationship to our fellows. And the gateway into this ethical area is a fitting relationship with fathers and mothers.

It's not by chance that the Bible speaks first of parents. Honoring father and mother comes before not killing and not committing adultery. One who has never learned to obey this first moral imperative lovingly has difficulty with those that follow. For how can we truly love our neighbors if we cannot truly love our own fathers and mothers?

The fifth commandment places parents as the primary authority under God—and our main case study, "Please, Won't You Call?" deals with a parent/child relationship that probes issues of love, parental responsibility, and honor. Can Megan honor her father and yet not respond to his request to return his calls? Does the father's neglect justify his daughter's rejection?

The fifth commandment also makes parents the symbols of all other authority. Our alternate case, "Players Say No to Coach," looks at the issue of honoring and respecting one of the many "others" God has placed over us. In both case studies, the demands of "honor" may seem quite clear to you (though perhaps a bit less clear to the teens you teach). Use the case study of your choice to look together at exactly what it means to honor parents and others in authority.

In Hebrew, the word *honor* literally means *heavy*. To honor someone is to make them "heavy," to give them weight. That doesn't refer, of course, to body weight, but to dignity and respect. In a similar way the Bible speaks of honoring and glorifying God. We should make God heavy, for the weight of glory is the respect due to the Creator of heaven and earth, the Ruler of the universe.

To honor parents and others in authority is to respect them, to give them weight in our lives, to let them influence us. Parents, in particular, must be obeyed, honored, and loved. We should listen respectfully to their words and speak well of them. Whoever curses parents or speaks ill of them, says the Old Testament, deserves death (Ex. 21:17). So ignoring aging parents, being obviously impatient with their foibles, wincing at their remarks are all acts of dishonor. Sullen obedience, sneering jokes, or lifted eyebrows all make light of parents (or others in authority) and fail to give them proper weight.

The Heidelberg Catechism expands the meaning of the commandment to include being patient with the failings of our parents. That's a good line to keep in mind as you discuss "Please, Won't You Call?" Parents, on the other hand, are responsible before God to care for and love their children, to teach them about the Lord, to spend time with them, to discipline them in love, to avoid "exasperating" them (Eph. 6:4).

Honoring our parents is one of God's commands. It is an ethical principle basic to family living, an explicit *ought* that remains constant even when ways of obeying it change drastically. Consider, for a moment, how honoring parents continues to rule our moral behavior through incredibly altered life situations. At one life stage, literal obedience may be required. At another, it may be impossible or unwise. Parents may demand something that their mature "child" judges to be wrong. Or they may, by their misbehavior or mistreatment of their offspring, force children to find ways to honor them that include a loving rebuke or correction. But honor them we must. That's God's clear command.

God has promised length of days (Ex. 20:12) and well-being (Deut. 5:16) to those who honor their parents. This does not necessarily mean each individual who honors his or her parents will enjoy a wealthy and healthy old age. Rather, it's a covenantal promise of a joyous future for God's faithful people. The Old Testament extended this promise to all the commandments (Deut. 5:33; Ps. 91:15-16; Isa. 53:10). Length of days in the promised land, joy, and salvation are given to those who keep all God's statutes. But emphatically this reward is given to those who honor their parents. Obeying and listening to father and mother prepare us to follow the blessed ways of life. By honoring parents, we learn wisdom (Prov. 4:1-5) and establish the foundation for law-abiding, coventantly faithful living.

This commandment teaches a normative attitude toward parents, toward all authorities, and toward all people. Honoring parents is the first way in which we "love our neighbors as ourselves," the first of the acts of loving obedience we owe to each other.

—HAS

LEADING THE SESSION

1 Role Plays: To Honor or Not to Honor
Materials: Bible, newsprint, markers

Give someone your Bible and ask him or her to read the fifth commandment from Exodus 20:12: "Honor your father and your mother, so that you may live long in the land the LORD your God is giving you." Explain briefly that the Bible extends this "honor" to include not just parents but all persons whom God has placed in authority over us (police officers, teachers, employers, coaches, elders, pastors, and so on). "Everyone must submit himself to the governing authorities, for there is no authority except that which God has established" (Rom. 13:1).

Divide the class into groups of two or three and ask half of the groups to role-play a situation that shows someone their age *honoring* their parent(s) or someone else in authority. Ask the remaining groups to role-play a situation that shows someone their age *dishonoring* their parent(s) or someone else in authority. Role plays should be brief—not longer than a minute each. Give the groups five minutes to prepare their role plays.

When the groups are ready, begin with the role plays that show dishonor to parents or someone else in authority. Then switch to the role plays that show honor.

After watching both sets of role plays, attempt to define what it means to honor parents and others in authority. Jot down student responses on a sheet of newsprint. Here are some ideas they may come up with:

■ to love them (in the case of parents, at least)

■ to obey them (cheerfully!)

TIP
Do not attempt to define "honor" or "dishonor" for the small groups. If students ask, explain that you'd like them to use the role plays to demonstrate their understanding of what the words mean. The idea is to see how students interpret the commandment. Encourage creativity and humor.

61

TIP

You may want to
share the explana-
tion of honor given
in the Session
Background: "mak-
ing heavy, giving
weight to."

- to respect them

- to appreciate them

- to say good things about them

- to be loyal to them

- to be patient and understanding when they fail

- to submit to their correction and discipline

When you've got a good list, ask: **In what situations might it be difficult to honor a parent or other person in authority?**

Listen to their comments, and point out that today's case study, "Please, Won't You Call?" deals with such a situation.

---

option: alternative to role plays

If don't have enough students for several role plays, or if your students don't enjoy them, try this instead. Bring a roll of paper to class (the kind used for tablecloths) and supply students with markers. Ask them to sketch or describe situations that show honor and dishonor to parents and others in authority. Review the results, then pick up step 1 at the point immediately after the role plays.

---

2 Case Study: Please, Won't You Call?
Materials: Resource Page: "Fifth Commandment" (one copy per student, p. 135), Case Study Card: "Please, Won't You Call?" (or alternate: "Players Say No to Coach"), newsprint, markers, pens

Distribute today's case study, "Please, Won't You Call?" along with the resource page (the suggested approach combines the usual Bible study with the case study in one step). If you choose the alternate case, see the option on page 64.

Read the case to the class, then give students five minutes or more of quiet time to read the resource page. Ask them to underline words or phrases that seem to support Megan's saying yes to her father's request (such as, "that I be patient with their failings"). Ask them to circle items that seem to support Megan's saying no to her father's request (such as, "don't neglect your children").

When all are finished, divide into groups of three or four students each and ask the groups to decide what Megan should do. Should she honor her father by agreeing to respond to his phone calls?

Ask them to jot their recommendation and the reasons supporting it on a sheet of newsprint. Give the groups ten minutes to complete their task, then review their responses. Here are some things you may want to mention if students don't:

Reasons to respond to her father's phone calls (or find other ways to communicate):

- This would be a legitimate way to honor her dad, something God wants us to do.

- The fifth commandment does not say parents need to earn our respect and honor.

- Her dad says he loves her and wants to know about her life.

- He's obviously sincere.

- He's apologized for past neglect.

- Megan once loved her dad and probably still does.

- Nobody's perfect—parents or children. Megan should be a little more patient with her father's failures as a parent.

- Megan will be a better person if she can overcome her bitterness toward her dad.

- Megan has little to lose by saying yes to her dad's request.

Reasons not to respond to her father's phone calls (or to find other ways to communicate):

- Her dad has not paid much attention to Megan for many years. Why should she follow the advice in Ephesians 6:1-3 (to obey parents) when her dad has not followed verse 4 (don't exasperate your children)?

- He left home for another woman, causing Megan and her mother a lot of suffering.

- His job as a pilot permits only very limited communication with Megan. Even if he really wants to get involved with Megan's life, will he be able to do so?

- Megan has a new family. Her mother and her stepdad may resent her biological father butting in.

- People who neglect their kids for most of their lives aren't likely to change.

activity adaptation

For an individual approach (rather than a small group approach), have students imagine that Megan is a friend of theirs who has asked for their advice. Ask them to write her a short letter with their recommendation, including their reasons for it. Then ask several students to read their letters aloud.

TIP

The moral *ought* to honor parents may make resolving today's cases seem quite obvious to you. Megan ought to honor her father by accepting his request to return his calls; the new coach ought not to dishonor the old coach by allowing her team to wear the offensive T-shirts. Cut and dried, plain and simple. Be aware, however, that your students might not see it quite so clearly. Kids who have survived a divorce, for example, or who have a parent who hasn't paid much attention to them, might readily sympathize with Megan's reluctance to open communications with an "out of touch" dad who left his wife to raise a daughter alone. Or, in the alternate case, kids who have experienced the harsh discipline of an overzealous coach may well side with the team in defying his authority.

After the small groups report, ask a couple of summary question along these lines:

- **How many of you agree (show of hands) that Megan's father deserves to be honored by his daughter?**

- **How many of you agree (show of hands) that Megan needs to honor her father, whether or not he deserves it?** It's important that students recognize the moral *ought* of honoring parents. We have no choice in this. It's a direct command from God. We must honor our parents, whether or not they deserve such honor. Of course, parents must be responsible before God and loving to their children, but if they are not, children must still honor them. Megan needs to honor her father.

- **How might Megan honor her father?** Use this question to get at the idea that "honoring" can take different forms in different situations. In Megan's case, for example, the most obvious way to honor her father would be to do as he requested and answer his calls. But maybe your students can suggest other ways that Megan could honor her dad; for instance, she might agree to write him a letter from time to time or to see him now and then. Or she might explain (kindly!) that she needs time to think about her response.

- **In what situations might you honor a parent—or someone else in authority—by disobeying him or her?** One example is when parents ask us to do something that's clearly wrong in God's sight; for example, if they ask us to lie to a teacher about being sick so the family can leave early on a vacation. Another instance is when a parent is not in control of his or her own life due to the debilitating effects of alcohol, drug abuse, or emotional illness. Such a parent might make an irrational demand that we disobey out of concern for the parent's welfare.

Please point out that exceptions to this command are just those—exceptions.

Give the group a minute to share what they think Megan decided, then explain that she remained opposed to communicating with her dad. To date, she's had no further contact with him. Unfortunately, Megan's inability to deal with her anger at her dad causes her to act out in a number of self-destructive ways involving sex and alcohol.

TIP

"Honoring" parents may well be repulsive to young people who have suffered abuse. Although your students may not have been abused, they may know others who have, so the issue is worth bringing up. Stress that it is essential to tell a counselor (or someone else who can help) about such abuse, even though it might bring public shame to the parent. This does not violate the fifth commandment. Honoring God may involve dishonoring people.

option: alternate case study: players say no to coach

Today's alternate case study takes the fifth commandment beyond the familiar confines of honoring parents to honoring others whom God has placed in authority over us. If you choose this case, you'll want to emphasize the "other authorities" aspect of the commandment in step 1. Have some students role-play honoring and dishonoring someone other than a parent who has authority over them. Have students list ways to honor and respect not only parents but others in authority.

Use the resource sheet selectively, reading Exodus 20:12, Romans 13:1 and Q&A 104.

To discuss the case, divide into groups of three to five students each. Have half of the groups list all the reasons they can think of why Ms. Kruzman ought to say no to her team wearing the "Under New Management" T-shirts. Have the other half list all the reasons they can think of why she ought to say yes. Allow up to ten minutes for this activity. Have the groups write their responses on sheets of newsprint. Review the responses together and ask questions to bring out any reasons that the groups may have missed.

Sample responses for saying no:

- Wearing the T-shirts would be disrespectful to the previous coach.
- Team members had behaved badly and deserved to be punished.
- Mr. Acre had not abused his authority in telling his team to run; most of the parents and the media supported his action.
- Team members were too used to getting their way—they needed the discipline of being told no.
- Saying no would affirm a basic ethical principle of honoring those in authority.
- Saying no would avoid negative publicity for the school, the coach, and the team.

Sample responses for saying yes:

- Mr. Acre may have been guilty of abusing his authority by his alleged emotional outbursts and by not being "democratic."
- The offense of the team members against the rival team was relatively mild and not malicious, according to the coach himself.
- Team members (supposedly) offered to run the next day.
- The lettering on the shirts was small (said the new coach), and not many spectators at the state tournament would know what was being referred to.
- Saying no would get Ms. Kruzman off to a very bad start with her new team.

Call for a vote on the issue, then explain what actually happened in this case. Ms. Kruzman allowed the printing of the shirts. As it turned out, the slogan "Under New Management" was plain to observers at the state tournament. The sportswriters who attended knew about the coach's resignation. After the tournament they blasted the school, Ms. Kruzman, and the principal in their newspapers. The principal said he didn't see anything wrong with the shirts. The sports writers thought Seaholm should voluntarily withdraw from fielding a tennis team for one year.

Here's an interesting follow-up question to the case: **What should you do if you find yourself in a situation where someone in authority actually does abuse that authority in some way?**

3 Writing: Letter to Parents or Others in Authority

Materials: writing paper, pens; optional: resource page

Invite your students to write a short letter of appreciation to their parents or to a teacher, pastor, coach, employer, or other adult. The intent of the letter is to honor such persons with a sincere letter of thanks and appreciation. The more specific the letters are, the better ("I really appreciate the way you took time to help me with my Spanish homework last semester"; "Thank you for being someone I can count on to listen, like the time when . . ."). The letters are to be completely private, between the student and the person(s) who will receive the letter.

---

activity adapation

To broaden the activity, ask students for examples of other ways (besides notes of appreciation) in which they could honor their parents or others in authority. The role plays at the beginning of the session might be the source of some good ideas. Encourage students to commit to one specific way of showing honor to a parent or someone else this week.

Your students may need more time to finish the letters. If so, encourage them to finish the letters today at home. If presenting the letter to the person(s) they're writing to seems threatening or embarrassing, students can simply explain that the letters were written as part of their study of the fifth commandment at church.

Close the session with a time of silence, during which students may thank God for their parent(s) (or others in authority) and ask for guidance and help in honoring them. You may wish to close the prayer time by inviting students to read Q&A 104 with you from the resource page.

the sixth commandment

SESSION FOCUS

The sixth commandment requires us to respect human life because it is from God. Humans alone are formed in God's image. Therefore, we are not to take another's life, except in self-defense or in a just war. And we are always to show love for one another.

SCRIPTURE

Exodus 20:13; Genesis 1:26-27; 9:6; Job 10:12; Psalm 8:5-6; 119:73; 139:13-14; Isaiah 46:4; Matthew 25:40; 26:52; Luke 6:36; John 1:3-4; 3:16; Romans 13:3-4; 1 Corinthians 6:20; James 2:1, 5, 8-9, 12-13

SESSION GOALS

- ■ to give biblical reasons for the sacredness of human life

- ■ to apply the sixth commandment and other biblical guidelines to a case involving the issue of capital punishment

- ■ to affirm the worth of each person in the class

SESSION AT A GLANCE

Learning Activity	Materials	Time
1. *Pictures: The Value of Life.* We look at pictures affirming life and the joy of living, then read the sixth commandment.	Pictures clipped from newspapers or magazines that suggest life and the joy of living—at least two for every student, tape, posterboard or newsprint	10 minutes
2. *Bible Study: Why Human Life Is Sacred.* Pairs face each other, then find reasons in Scripture why they should value and respect each other as human beings.	Resource Page: "Fifth Commandment" (one copy per student, p. 137), paper, pens	10-15 minutes
3. *Case Study:* Texas v. Karla Faye Tucker. Small groups become "lawyers" arguing for and against a stay of execution for Karla Faye. (Alternate case and discussion approach provided.)	Resource Page: "Fifth Commandment," Case Study Card: *"Texas v. Karla Faye Tucker"* (or alternate: "Who Has the Heart for Brian?"), paper, pens	20-25 minutes
4. *Affirmation: You Are . . .* We jot down positive qualities that we see in each person in class, then pray for each person by name.	Notecards or small slips of paper, pens	10 minutes

SESSION BACKGROUND

In this session you'll be teaching the difference between the popular "reverence for life" and the biblical "sanctity of life" ethical principles. The first is a humanistic moral principle exalted into an entire life ethic. The second is a God-given imperative to respect God-given life as part of our loving obedience to God and our obedient love to our neighbor. The difference lies not necessarily in how much life is treasured (here a good humanitarian may outdo a poor Christian). Rather, the difference is the reason for valuing life and the Christian insistence that love, not life, has first priority.

"Reverence for life" is a term from Albert Schweitzer. That great German musician, medic, and missionary took ideas from another great man, Mahatma Ghandi, and developed them into an ethical regard for all living beings. In a day when most Westerners ruthlessly and callously butchered, mutilated, and exploited their world, he demanded a caring, careful handling of all creatures. Today the threat of terrorism or a nuclear holocaust or a polluted planet has encouraged a Western generation to make preserving life the one ethical absolute. From the minute water creature endangered by a new dam to the condemned murderer on death row, all the living are considered to have an inalienable right to exist. Life is good, the great good.

"Sanctity of life" also recognizes life's goodness. God declared it so. But life is to be valued *because* it's God's gift. God is the Lord of life; therefore no one may lightly regard, selfishly treat, or carelessly take life from any of God's creatures. But especially human life, which reflects the image of God, is sacred. The Bible expressly forbids the shedding of *human* blood, "for God made man in his own image" (Gen. 9:6).

Humankind, then, in Christian ethics, possesses a unique worth above all other living beings. Humans have an alien dignity, a claim to respect conferred by the God who values them so highly he sent Christ to die for them.

Our life, and our neighbor's life, is a loan, a trust, a gift held in stewardship. It's not ours to end if we get more tired of living than afraid of dying. A fetus is not the mother's possession to keep or kill at her convenience. I have no right to control, alter, or end another's life without answering to God for what I do. "You shall not murder" is the command of the life-giving God.

Our main case study *("Texas v. Carla Faye Tucker")* raises the question of exceptions. Is killing ever justifiable? To that we must answer yes. The sixth commandment forbids willful, malicious taking of life—what we rightly call murder. But it does not forbid the power of the sword (Rom. 13:4). Taking of life by means of capital punishment, war, or police action may all be justified. How so? Because, says the Heidelberg Catechism, "prevention of murder is also why government is armed with the sword" (Answer 105). Government power is intended to protect people from violence and hurt. The state should use force for justice, so that under an equitable rule human life can develop as God wills. A just war is meant to prevent destruction. Self-defense is meant to preserve life.

Still, Christians differ on some specific issues, including that of capital punishment. The case of Karla Faye Tucker adds an interesting complication in that a cold-blooded axe-murderer who was sentenced to death claimed to have found Christ and forgiveness during her time in prison. Because of the tremendous change in her life, she argued, and because she was no longer a menace to society, she should be pardoned, and, in a few years, set free. The case, which drew considerable attention from the media, was eventually decided by one man: Texas governor George W. Bush.

Our alternate case ("Who Has the Heart for Brian?") looks at the ethics involved in deciding who should—and who should not—be eligible for a heart transplant. Specifically, does a young man who is developmentally disabled and suffering from mild mental illness have the same right to a (rare) new heart as other patients without his limitations? Who decides—and on what basis—who is to live and who is left to die?

In challenging cases such as these, there are no easy answers. But Christian love frees us to be truly human *and* to be fully just. It frees us to obey not only the letter but also the spirit of God's demands. It enables us to treat our neighbors—no matter who they are—as we ourselves wish to be treated—in decency, justice, and love.

—HAS

LEADING THE SESSION

1 Pictures:
The Value of Life

Materials: pictures clipped from newspapers or magazines that suggest life and the joy of living—at least two for every student, tape, posterboard or newsprint

For this step, you'll need to do a bit of collecting prior to class. Look for photos in magazines or newspapers that depict or suggest life and the joy of living: a newborn child and mother, kids having fun, a wedding or other celebration, a triumphal moment in sports, a romantic scene, a rescue, a triumph over some challenge or obstacle, a portrait of a very old person smiling, and so on. Clip the photos and arrange them on a table or floor in your classroom. Be sure to have at least two or three photos for every student.

As students arrive, ask them to pick one photo from the table that they like, one that says something meaningful to them. One at a time, have them show their photos to the rest of the group and give a brief explanation of its appeal. When finished with their explanation, they should tape their photo to a posterboard or sheet of newsprint you've displayed on the wall or on a table.

Take a moment to look at all the photos and ask the class to suggest possible captions for the assembled display. Pick a caption or two that the group seems to like and label the display. Ask the class if they can guess what criterion you had in mind when you selected the pictures. Explain that you hoped the pictures suggested life itself and the joy of living. Point out that there are no photos in the display that depict death or defeat.

Bridge to the idea that today's session is about affirming the value of life, and human life in particular. As Christians we believe that human life is sacred and must be treated with the utmost care. Have someone read the sixth commandment from Exodus 20:13.

TIP
For small classes, you may want to have each student pick two photos instead of just one.

activity adaptation

Consider expanding your photo display to include photos depicting or suggesting death/dying. Display these pictures with the life-affirming photos and let students choose one or more that they find meaningful or that moves them in some way. After their explanations, discuss the two categories of photos and our strong desire to protect and celebrate life, even in circumstances that threaten it.

option: alternate opening: to die for?

No time to dig up those photos for step 1? Consider this easy alternative. Give students notecards as they arrive. When all are present, briefly introduce the idea of believing in something so much or caring about something so much that you'd be willing to give up your life for it, if necessary. Ask everyone to complete this sentence starter: **"I think I'd be willing to give up my life for . . ."** Invite sharing of responses and bridge to the idea that our lives are the most valuable possession we have been given by God. To give them up voluntarily for any reason is something most of us don't even want to think about, and something we hope we never have to do. Our lives are precious. That's why God protects human life with the sixth commandment. Have someone read it aloud.

2 Bible Study: Why Human Life is Sacred

Materials: paper, pen, Resource Page: "Sixth Commandment" (one copy per student, p. 137), newsprint, marker

Divide into pairs and have the pairs face sit facing each other. Give each pair a sheet of paper and a pen. Ask the pairs to look at each other—trying not to giggle—and to answer this question: **Why should I value and protect and respect your life?** Partners should work together to make a list of all the reasons they can think of. Let the pairs work for several minutes, jotting down their ideas.

Then give each person a person a copy of the resource page for the sixth commandment and encourage them to scan the passages [on side 1 and half of side 2, up to the heading "Additional Passages for the Case Studies"] for new ideas to add to their lists.

After another five minutes or so, have pairs read their list aloud. As the lists are read, summarize what's said on a sheet of newsprint (or on your board). Record any silly ideas ("Because you're cute!") along with the serious ones. Give every pair a chance to read their list.

When you've got a good master list on your newsprint or board, briefly describe the difference between the humanitarian idea of "reverence for life" with its belief that life has inherent value simply because it is life, and the Christian idea of "sanctity of life," with its belief that life has only conferred or bestowed worth because it is a gift from God. Please see the Session Background for details.

Ask students to take another look at the master list and to identify those statements that especially show this "sanctity of life" idea. Look for (or add to the list) statements like these:

- God values human life and forbids one human murdering another (Ex. 20:13).

- God values human life so much that God's only Son was sent to die to preserve it (John 3:16).

- God is the giver of all life; life is a gift from God (Gen. 1:26-27; Job 10:12, Ps. 119:73; 139:13-14; Isa. 46:4; John 1:3-4).

- All humans are made in the image of God and so are crowned with dignity and honor (Gen. 1:26-27; Ps. 8:5).

- Humans are unique; of all creatures they are the only ones with whom God enters a covenantal relationship; they rule over the rest of creation (Ps. 8:6).

- We are not our own, but belong to our Savior, Jesus Christ. Our lives are on loan from God. We cannot do with them as we wish but must treat all human life with respect and care (1 Cor. 6:20).

Leave the newsprint sheets on display for the remainder of the session.

3 Case Study:
Texas v. Karla Faye Tucker
Materials: Resource Page: "Sixth Commandment," Case Study Card: "Texas v. Karla Faye Tucker" (or alternate: "Who Has the Heart for Brian?"), paper, pens

Distribute today's case study ("Texas v. Karla Faye Tucker"). Have students keep their resource page handy as well. Comment that the case involves an unusual twist on the capital punishment issue, one that caused a lot of debate and interest in the national media. Read the case to the class.

Divide the class into two teams of "lawyers" who are arguing Karla Faye's case before the Board of Pardons, represented by you (the leader).

One team will argue that Karla Faye ought to be granted a stay of execution; the other team will argue that she should not. Their job is to convince you of their point of view. They should use the case study itself plus any material on the resource page they think is pertinent to their case (call attention to the Bible passages on side 2 under the heading "Additional Passages . . ."). Their arguments may include debating the legitimacy of capital punishment itself, if they wish.

TIP

Ask your students not to reveal how the case turned out, if they happen to know. Knowing the verdict ahead of time would make the case less fun and less interesting to discuss for the rest of the class. If students guess that the Texas governor mentioned in the case is George W. Bush, just say that information isn't important to know right now. Later, they'll find out who decided the case and how it was resolved.

TIP

Check out the optional approach to this case if your class has more than a dozen students or less than four.

TIP

Tell students that you're aware that the case was not argued by teams of lawyers before the Board of Pardon (although the one lawyer who argued for a stay of execution probably wished he had a whole team with him!). Our staging of teams of lawyers is just a way to get at the issues in the case and have some fun doing so.

TIP

Don't worry if all this back and forth stuff breaks down. Better to let the "laywers" be enthusiastic in presenting their case than in settling for orderly but dreary presentations. Be flexible. To pull things together at the end, you could ask each team to pick someone to summarize their case for the Board in one minute or less.

Give the groups ten minutes to prepare their case. They should outline their main arguments and divide up presenting their case between the team members. Teams can select a name for their team if they wish and have an informal cheering section too.

When the teams are ready, have the opposing "lawyers" sit on opposite sides of the room. You (representing the Board) should take a position between the two teams. Explain that you will first allow the team speaking *against* a stay of execution to present one of its key points (the student making the point may stand up to speak); you will then give the opposing team a chance to rebut the point. Let the team speaking against a stay of execution work through all their arguments. Then reverse, letting the team *in favor of* a stay of execution present all its arguments, with the other team rebutting each point as they wish. You may want to have someone from each team summarize the team's case at the end.

After hearing all the arguments for and against a stay of execution, ask a couple of questions along these lines:

■ **Do you agree that Christians can legitimately differ on the issue of capital punishment in general? Why or why not?**

If your students are Christian Reformed, you may want to note that the synod (governing body) of the Christian Reformed Church took the following stance on capital punishment: "Modern states are not obligated by Scripture, creed, or principle to institute and practice capital punishment. . . . However, Scripture acknowledges the right of modern states to institute and practice capital punishment if it is exercised with utmost restraint" (*Doctrinal and Ethical Positions,* Christian Reformed Church in North America).

■ **What, if anything, might make you as a Christian support the death penalty in a specific case?** Students may cite such things as the extent and nature of the crime itself, a lack of remorse on the part of the person who committed the crime, the threat to society if that person were ever paroled or escaped prison.

■ **What are some wrong motives or reasons for supporting the death penalty?** Revenge or vengeance is not a suitable motive for a Christian (see Rom. 12:19). Neither is the idea that putting someone to death costs less than keeping him or her in prison for life (in fact, it may cost more, due to the high cost of appeals, but that's not the issue here—the issue is that human life is always more important than dollars). An interesting side question: Suppose that capital punishment deters others from committing similar crimes (though it hasn't been shown to do that). Is deterrence a legitimate reason for capital punishment?

Conclude by telling the "lawyers" that the Board of Pardons can't make up its mind in this case, so it's now all up to the governor. Ask the students to imagine themselves in the governor's position. Pass out slips of paper and have the students mark yes to indicate Karla Faye should be pardoned or no to indicate she should not. Collect the slips and announce the verdict.

Tell the class that the governor of Texas at the time, George W. Bush, denied the pardon, saying that he based his decision strictly on two questions: Did she commit the crime? And did she get a fair trial? At 6:00 p.m. on February 3, 1998, Karla Faye Tucker was executed by lethal injection.

option: alternate to lawyer approach

After reading the case to the class, ask them to imagine that they are the governor who must make the decision about Karla's appeal. Distribute paper ask them to write their verdict and defend it, telling why they decided as they did. Have them read their letters aloud. Summarize their arguments on two sheets of newsprint, one labeled "For the pardon" the other "Against the pardon." Use the questions at the end of the regular step to wrap up the discussion.

option: alternate case study: who has the heart for Brian?

Read the case, then ask students to imagine they are on the University of Washington medical team that must decide whether or not Brian should be placed on a waiting list for a new heart. Divide into small groups and give the groups ten minutes to reach a decision. They should jot their decision and supporting reasons on a sheet of newsprint. Ask them to be sure to look at the biblical principles involved, using the resource page.

(If you have a small class or prefer not to work in groups, lead the entire class in the above exercise, recording their ideas on two sheets of newsprint posted on your wall. You may want to let two students do the actual writing on the newsprint while you led the discussion.)

Review the responses of the small groups, asking questions to bring out any arguments they may have omitted. Sample responses:

Reasons *for* placing Brian on the waiting list for a new heart:

- He urgently needs a heart to survive.

- He wants a new heart and is willing and eager to receive one.

- Brian, like all humans, is made in God's image (note supporting texts). No less than other humans, his life is precious and ought to be protected and preserved.

- Discriminating against Brian because of his physical and mental liabilities is the kind of favoritism James warns against (see resource sheet).

- Helping those who—for whatever reason—are less able to help themselves is a basic Christian principle (see *Our World Belongs to God* passage on resource sheet).

- Brian has demonstrated he can handle multiple medications of the kind he would require after surgery.

Reasons *against* placing Brian on the waiting list for a new heart:

- His doctors are concerned that he lacks the mental ability to handle all the complications resulting from the heart transplant.

- He demonstrated a certain amount of mental instability when previously hospitalized.

- His chances of surviving a heart transplant are probably not as good as someone without his physical and mental limitations.

- Giving Brian a new heart will mean that another patient—who might be better qualified to receive it—will die.

- An unanswered question is whether Brian has enough people to help him recover at home from the transplant operation and to supervise his medication, and so on.

- Medication rather than surgery might be a better alternative for Brian.

After reviewing your students' recommendations, you can tell them that the University of Washington Medical Center evaluated Brian's case for a year and a half, while treating him with medications. When he took a sudden turn for the worse, doctors agreed he clearly qualified medically for a transplant. The issue of post-surgical care was settled when a teacher agreed to assume his guardianship and provide home care. He was placed on a waiting list for a transplant. On September 11, 2001, a charter plane carrying his new heart had to be intercepted by an Air Force fighter, due to the grounding of all aircraft throughout the nation on that day (the day of the terrorist attacks). However, the heart was delivered and inserted within the allotted eight-hour time slot. At this printing, Brian Cortez is doing well with his new heart and a new life.

4 Affirmation: You Are . . .
Materials: notecards or small slips of paper, pens

Comment that the positive side of the sixth commandment causes us to look at each other—and all people—with respect. Rather than "killing" each other with unkind words or actions, we are to go out of our way to treat each other as imagebearers of God. We are to build each other up, not tear each other down.

Hand out notecards or small slips of paper to each student. Each person should receive as many notecards or slips of paper as the total number of persons in your class—so if there are six students, each gets six notecards or slips of paper.

Mention one of your students' names and ask each person to jot down one positive quality they see in that person (example: "You are a person who smiles a lot—I like that!").

Collect the notecards or slips of paper and give them to the person whose name was mentioned. Ask that the person receiving the comments not read them until everyone else has also received comments. Continue by mentioning another student's name and repeating the process, until each person has collected positive comments about him- or herself from every student in class.

Conclude by giving students a minute to read (silently) the comments written about them.

For your closing prayer, explain that the class will be praying silently for each student by name. Ask if students have any special concerns or items for praise that they'd like others to pray for. Then lead a time of guided prayer, along these lines:

Lord, we thank you for [name], a person made in your likeness. . . .

Pause a moment to give students time to pray silently, then continue with the name of another student. Conclude by thanking God for each member of your class and asking God's blessing on them as they attempt to treat others as imagebearers of God.

TIP
It's possible that some jokesters will say things about their peers that are less than complimentary, and that could, in fact, hurt. Please emphasize how easily our joking around can inflict real damage on others, and how we need to steer clear of any such temptation in this exercise.

the seventh commandment

SESSION FOCUS

The seventh commandment requires us to live within the limits of fidelity, purity, and decency that God has placed on expressing our God-given sexuality.

SCRIPTURE

Genesis 1:27-28, 31; 2:16-17; Exodus 20:14; Deuteronomy 24:5; Matthew 18:5-6; Romans 13:1; 1 Corinthians 6:19-20; 13:4-7, 13; Ephesians 5:3-4; 5:33; Colossians 3:18-21, 23

SESSION GOALS

- to give examples of myths about love and sex that our society promotes

- to identify basic biblical truths about our sexuality

- to discuss a case study about access to pornography in public libraries

- to pick some words to live by from Scripture or elsewhere and commit to letting them serve as a guide to our own sexuality

SESSION AT A GLANCE

Learning Activity	Materials	Time
1. *Speed Writing: Myths About Sex and Love.* Small groups race to write myths about sex and love that our culture, and especially the media, promote.	Paper (three to five dozen sheets), markers in one color, tape, Resource Page: "Seventh Commandment" (one copy per student, p. 139), optional: prizes for winning team	15 minutes
2. *Bible Study: Replacing Myths with Biblical Truths.* Small groups read Bible passages and other material to create lists of truths about sex and love.	Resource Page: "Seventh Commandment," paper (three to five dozen sheets), markers of a color that's different from the color used in step 1	20 minutes
3. *Case Study: To Filter Out Porn.* We create TV spots or print ads promoting or opposing filters on computers in a public library. (Alternate case and discussion approach provided.)	Resource Page: "Seventh Commandment," Case Study Card: "To Filter Out Porn" (or alternate: "Go Live with Your Mistress"), posterboard or newsprint, markers, small slips of paper for ballots	20 minutes
4. *Commitment: Words to Live By.* From the truth statements and/or Scripture we pick words to live by in the area of sexuality and love.	Notecards, resource page, pens	5 minutes

SESSION BACKGROUND

For Christians, the morality of sexuality should be open and clear. Our Christian ethical absolute should come to splendid expression in our sexual lives. Where else can we, must we, be so fully concerned, so aware of the needs of others, so sensitive to their feelings? Where else should we seek wholeheartedly the other's good, loving the other as ourselves? In the area of human sexuality we should be able to receive clear directions from Christian morality.

Yet sexuality is one area where Christians often find it especially difficult to give positive ethical direction. Christians tend to shy away from sexuality, finding it hard to talk about. While asserting that it's one of God's good gifts, we tend to set off our sexuality from the rest of our ethical living, fence it 'round with a few strict prohibitions, and then leave it as a domain of romantic love. Here, where ethical love should so properly control, a lower, erotic love often rules.

Such moral abandonment of human sexuality has left the typical Christian young person facing a false choice of two extremes: "if it feels good, do it" or look the other way and pretend sex doesn't exist. In old fashioned-terms, be a playboy/girl or be a prude.

We know all too well the extreme that's promoted by TV, advertising, movies, and novels. "Sex is fun," says popular culture. "Enjoy it. You can free yourself, find yourself, and be yourself by indulging in sex. Forget old-fashioned, moralistic hang-ups. Sex is natural and good. Try it!" Those who freely indulge are pictured as prettier, healthier, and happier than "moral" people.

Parts of the Christian community occasionally overreact to that distorted picture, sending out a strident message that the world reads as repression and even denial. Human sexuality is reduced to one word: *no.* Some of your students may be among those who wrongly suppose that a prudish attitude toward sex is the proper Christian response.

In today's session, you'll have an opportunity to discuss this and other myths about sexuality, as well as a Christian approach to the subject. Sex, of course, is a good gift from God. In it and by it we should praise God. Like other aspects of moral living, it has its proper limits: as God's gift of life is enjoyed within limits of respect for our neighbor's life and dignity, and as God's gift of property within limits of sharing and stewardship, so God's gift of sex is meant to be practiced within marriage bonds. When the boundary of faithfulness to one partner is respected, it becomes an area where we experience the fullest human communion and the deepest enduring love, an area where can freely glorify our God.

Our alternate case ("Go Live with Your Mistress") deals with this principle of faithfulness in marriage, not in the context of an adulterous sexual affair but in the context of unfaithfulness at home caused by a husband's love affair with his job. That kind of unfaithfulness can destroy a marriage and a family just as readily as a sexual misadventure. It's a good lesson for your students to learn *before* marriage vows are exchanged.

In numerous places (see resource page) the Bible tells us that God wants decent, chaste lives from married and single persons. The Bible condemns all *porneia* (sexual looseness) for those who are and who are not married. Impurity and indecency are not fit for Christ's followers (Eph. 5:3-5). Our actions, looks, talk, thoughts, and desires must all be chaste. We are, body and soul, temples of the Holy Spirit; thus we must be clean and holy. Because we belong, body and soul, to our faithful Savior Jesus Christ, we long not for the perverse but the good, not for the dirty but the pure. Our sexuality also is part of the life we live for Christ.

When you discuss the main case study ("To Filter Out Porn"), your students will quickly see that it deals with an area (pornography) that the Bible condemns. No Christian can rightly argue for viewing porn on the Internet or anywhere else, and a good case can be made for fighting pornography wherever it can be found, including public libraries. What complicates this case is the issue of freedom of speech guaranteed by the first amendment to the constitution of the United States, to which all public institutions are bound, and which Christians too must respect (Rom. 13:1).

Throughout today's session, your students should see that our sexual behavior is never just limited to two people. That's an illusion. Everything we do has to do with God. Our Lord stands as a third party, not between us but above us—the guarantor of our vows, the judge of our failures, the forgiver of our sins, and the one whose grace makes gracious and good relationships possible. So whatever we do in this life area must fit who we are before God and who our God is. It must be holy, for the Spirit within us is holy. It must be good, for God demands goodness. It must be loving, for God loves.

—HAS

LEADING THE SESSION

1 Speed Writing: Myths About Sex and Love

Materials: paper (three to five dozen sheets), markers in one color, tape, Resource Page: "Seventh Commandment" (one copy per student, p. 139), optional: prizes for winning team

Distribute the resource page and ask for volunteers to read the seventh commandment, the quotes from the Heidelberg Catechism, and the stanza from *Our World Belongs to God.* Call attention to the line "sexuality is distorted in our fallen world." Comment that for the next few minutes we'll focus on myths about sexuality and love that our culture, especially the media, promotes. Ask them to put the resource page aside for a few minutes.

Divide into teams of two to four students each and give each team a couple of dozen sheets of plain paper and markers of one color, such as black or green (the reason for all the markers being the same color is to differentiate the myth statements from the truth statements in the next step). Ask the teams to write one "myth" about sexuality and love on each sheet of paper. Teams must tape the sheets of paper together to form one long display. After five minutes, the team with the longest display wins. Teams should tape their list to the wall or display it on a table or the floor.

Call time and compare the length of the taped-together displays (you may want to award a fun prize to team members with the longest display). Then have someone from each team read the myths his or her team came up with. Here are some things your students might mention (if necessary, you could run some of these by students to see if they agree the statements are myths):

TIP
Take care throughout today's session not to project a judgmental attitude about sex that your students may expect of people who are older than they are. We do tend to identify sex and youth, and your students know that. Emphasize that these myths apply to people of just about all ages, not only the young.

TIP
You may want to use same-gender groups for this activity. Doing so will also give you an opportunity to compare the myths suggested by males and by females. If the groups need help, suggest they think in terms of what our culture, especially the media, says is OK and is not OK. Give an example or two from the list below, if needed.

- Christians have a prudish attitude about sex.

- It's normal to have sex before marriage, abnormal not to.

- People who have a casual attitude toward sex have more fun than people who restrict sex to marriage.

- If you're in love, it's OK to have sex.

- Sex is the most important part of a relationship or marriage.

- God does not approve of our sexuality.

- Sex and love don't have to go together.

- There are no costs to sex, as long as protection is used.

- All men want is sex.

- All women want is love.

- Porn is harmless fun.

- Life is meaningless without sex.

- There's one perfect person for everyone.

- Physical appearance is the key to happiness.

- It's OK to break up a marriage if one's personal happiness is at stake.

- Divorce is normal, acceptable.

- Personal happiness and fulfillment is most important.

Leave the myths on display for the next step of the session. Collect the markers.

---

activity adaptation

If, for whatever reason, you prefer not to have students work in small groups, have them work individually to list (on separate sheets of paper) myths about sex. Collect and shuffle the papers, read each one aloud, and attach it to the wall or arrange on a table or the floor. This gives shy students a chance to contribute without others knowing what they wrote. Another possibility is simply to lead the entire class in a discussion of myths about sexuality and love, recording their responses on newsprint.

TIP
Can't find enough markers of the same color? An alternative is to use lightly colored sheets of paper to use for this step. The "truth statements" will then contrast nicely with the myths from the previous step.

2 Bible Study: Replacing Myths with Biblical Truths
Materials: Resource Page: "Seventh Commandment," paper (three to five dozen sheets), markers of a color that's different from the color used in step 1

Have students remain in the same teams or, for variety, form new teams of two to four students each. Distribute fresh sheets of paper to the groups, along with markers of a different color so that the "truth statements" stand out from the myths. Explain the activity, as follows.

- This time the teams have ten minutes to list "truth statements" about sexuality and love that they as Christians believe and affirm.

- These statements may often be the opposite of the myths that are on display from step 1, so teams should check the myth statements for ideas.

- The resource page for the seventh commandment is another good source of ideas.

- Statements should be expressed positively as much as possible (challenge teams to write them as catchy slogans, if they wish).

- Teams should list one idea per page of paper. This time they should *not* tape the pages together as in the previous step but just stack them off to one side.

- No race this time to get the most responses.

After ten minutes, ask the teams to take their "truth statements" and tape them over any specific "myths" that they refute. Not every myth statement need be covered, of course. If teams have truth statements that don't correct a specific myth, or if teams have duplicate truth statements, they may display these statements separately, off to one side of the myth statements.

Have team members take turns reading their truth statements. When possible, refer to the resource page for support of the statements. Sample responses follow:

- Sex—God's good gift to people.

- Male and female—the way God created us.

- Sex is good and meant to be enjoyed—God made it that way.

- Sex is meant for marriage only.

- Sex without love is cheap.

- There's more to marriage than sex!

- Sex is more than skin-deep.

- Your body is a temple—keep it holy.

- Porn pollutes.

- Wanted: men and women who respect each other.

- Waiting (until marriage) works!

- Faithfulness makes life worth living.

- "The greatest of these is love."

If you wish, have students remove the myths (that haven't been covered), leaving only the truth statements on display. Summarize by having someone read stanza 47 from *Our World Belongs to God* once again.

3 **Case Study:**
To Filter Out Porn

Materials: Resource Page: "Seventh Commandment," Case Study Card: "To Filter Out Porn" (or alternate: "Go Live with Your Mistress"), posterboard or newsprint, markers, small slips of paper for ballots

Distribute the case study "To Filter Out Porn" (for the alternate case, please see the second option on page 84). Ask someone to read the case aloud to the class.

Point out that both sides spent over $50,000 on this issue. Ask the class to imagine that they are Christian marketers who have been asked to come up with TV spots or print ads for or against the filters. Divide once more into small groups of two to five students each. Ask half the groups to design a creative TV spot or print ad *in favor of* the filters, the other half *against* the filters. The groups may assume that their audience is largely Christian, so it's a good idea to cite the Bible or refer to Christian principles.

Supply posterboard or newsprint sheets and markers to groups who want to do a print ad. Groups doing a TV spot really don't need any props (if they do, ask them to use imaginary props). Give the groups about ten minutes to invent a print ad or a TV spot.

Enjoy the TV productions and print ads! Afterward, you can answer any questions the class has about the case (except how it came out) and talk a bit about which biblical principles apply. Then hand out slips of paper for ballots and ask students to mark the ballots "yes" if they favor the filters and "no" if they oppose them. Count the ballots and compare the decision of the class to how the issue was actually resolved. Explain that Julie was among the 4,379 voters who turned down the filters in the city of Holland, Michigan, on February 22, 2000. Voting for the filters were 3,626 voters. Months later the library board again considered buying filters but decided not to install them.

---

option: alternate approach to main case

If you prefer a more straightforward approach to the case, work with the class to first list all the reasons against the filters, then all the reasons for them. Have a couple of students record the reasons on sheets of newsprint as they are given.

Sample reasons *against* the filters:

- The library reported few, if any, problems with children viewing porn on their computers.

- Installing the software might well violate the first amendment's protection of free speech. The library is a public institution and thus must answer to the government. Christians too must respect the authority of the government to protect the rights of its citizens (see Rom. 13:1).

- It's impossible to shield children from all the evils of our culture.

- God did not attempt to "censor" evil in the Garden of Eden. Adam and Eve, and all people since then, have to choose between good and evil (Gen. 2:16-17).

- Protecting the rights of some should not result in curtailing the rights of others.

- It's up to parents, not public institutions, to teach their children what's right and wrong.

- Concerned parents can either accompany their children to the library or have them do their research on home computers.

Sample reasons *in favor of* the filters:

- Porn is evil—it has no educational or artistic value. Christians especially need to oppose it everywhere they can, while staying within the limits of the law (Eph. 5:3-4).

- Children who are innocently exposed to porn or who deliberately access it can be harmed by it. Christians especially need to be sure that little ones aren't led into sin (Matt. 18:5-6).

- The first amendment protects free speech but does not protect providing obscene material to children (what's "obscene" is debatable, but it's usually defined as "material that appeals to a prurient interest in sex, is patently offensive, and lacks serious literary, artistic, political or scientific value").

- Adults who insist on unfiltered access to the Internet have one computer available for that purpose in the library (federal law).

- People who don't want to see porn should be protected from accidentally stumbling across it on the Internet.

- The library restricts printed material generally regarded as pornographic—why not restrict porn on the Internet?

When you've got two good lists similar to the above, take a sample vote, as suggested in the regular step.

alternate case study: go live with your mistress

Read the case and ask what in the world this has to do with the seventh commandment against adultery (it may not be all that obvious to students!). Infidelity to a marriage partner is the issue here, of course. Has Henry, as his wife accuses him, made a mistress out of his job? As the session background points out, that kind of unfaithfulness can destroy a marriage and a family just as readily as a sexual misadventure.

Ask other questions along these lines:

- **What is Henry's dilemma?**

- **What's good about Henry's dedication to his job? What's not so good?**

- **How many of you know someone with a parent like Henry? Have you been able to see any impact on that person's family?**

- **How do the Bible passages on the resource page (Deut. 24:5; Col. 3:18-22; Eph. 5:33) apply to this case?** You may want to call attention to the interesting progression in the Colossians passage. First, marriage partners owe love and respect to each other; then they need to be concerned about the children; and finally, work enters the picture. That's putting things in the right order, getting our priorities straight!

- **How many of you think there is a clear, moral *ought* in this case? If so, what would it be? How could it be accomplished?** Clearly, Henry needs to find some way to balance his work and his life at home, and the sooner the better. See if the class thinks along these lines. Then discuss some ways that Henry could resolve his dilemma.

Ask the class what they think Henry finally did. You can tell them that he thought about resigning from his job and discussed that option with his wife. However, they decided Henry should continue doing the job he loves so much but back off on some of his "after school" obligations so that he could spend more time at home. That is, in fact, what Henry has done.

4 Commitment: Words to Live By
Materials: notecards, resource page, pens

Take a moment to make a very important point: When we go beyond the boundaries that God has placed around human sexuality, when we "cross the line" and are feeling very guilty about what we've done, we need to remember that God forgives violations of the seventh commandment just as readily as violations of any other commandment. Once we ask forgiveness and decide to walk in God's way, there need be no lingering guilt. God gives us a brand-new, fresh start! Be sure your students hear this message today.

Continue by handing out one notecard to each student. Ask them to reflect quietly for a couple of minutes on this question: **Are there any "words to live by" in the statements of truth or on the resource page or elsewhere in Scripture that could guide you in the area of your own sexuality?** Give students time to select a phrase or sentence and write it on their notecards. Invite them to commit to and share their "words to live by" with the group, if they wish to do so.

End the session with a time of silent prayer, during which students may give thanks for God's gift of sexuality and ask God to bless the commitment they just made. Ask them to take their notecards home and look at them from time to time as a reminder of how God wants them to use the good gift of sexuality.

---

option: alternate ending

First Corinthians 13 presents a beautiful and challenging statement of what our love for others should be like. Have students read the passage responsively, alternating verses between two groups. Then give students a moment to pick one phrase that describes love from this passage (for example, "love keeps no record of wrongs"). Have them write the phrase on a notecard, then write the name of one person to whom they will attempt to show this kind of love this week, along with a specific way they could do this (for example, "not to hold a grudge against my friend Cindy for flirting with my boyfriend"). Close with a time of silent prayer, during which students may ask God's help in meeting their commitment.

the eighth commandment

SESSION FOCUS

The eighth commandment forbids us to steal outright, swindle our neighbors, want more than we need (greed) or waste God's gifts; it requires us to share with those in need.

SCRIPTURE

Exodus 20:15; Psalm 24:1; Matthew 7:12; Luke 12:13-21; 16:10; Ephesians 4:28

SESSION GOALS

- to describe what the eighth commandment forbids and what it requires

- to give biblical examples of violations of the eighth commandment

- to discuss a case involving a common form of theft

- to commit to an act of sharing and generosity

SESSION AT A GLANCE

Learning Activity	Materials	Time
1. *Presentations: The Many Faces of Theft.* We expand our ideas of what's prohibited by the eighth commandment by dramatizing examples of four types of theft, then list additional examples, and finally look at the positive side of the commandment.	Resource Page: "Eighth Commandment" (one copy per student, p. 143), pens, newsprint, marker	15 minutes
2. *Bible Study: The Rich Fool, Then and Now.* We read the Parable of the Rich Fool (Luke 12:13-21), then use our imaginations to complete a contemporary version of the parable.	Resource Page: "Eighth Commandment," pens	15 minutes
3. *Case Study: CDs for Tom and Thomas.* Working in groups, we list reasons for and against Tom's action in this case, then decide what he should do. (Alternate case and discussion approach provided.)	Resource Page: "Eighth Commandment," Case Study Card: "CDs for Tom and Thomas" (or alternate: "Slots or Not?"), newsprint, markers	20-25 minutes
4. *Closing: Commitment and Guided Prayer.* We commit to a specific way of sharing a small part of what God has given us, then ask for God's forgiveness and blessing.	Resource Page: "Eighth Commandment," pens	5 minutes

SESSION BACKGROUND

In four brief words, the eighth commandment presents an entire area of ethical endeavor—"You shall not steal." That simple, straightforward demand directs our moral attention to the whole realm of possessions and their use.

Clear though the command may be, Western society seems permeated by a disrespect for other's property rights. Outright theft may be less common than in earlier ages, but cheating of all kinds seems far more common. Tax fraud, shoplifting, expense-account padding, insurance deceptions, welfare cheats, customs smuggling, and classroom cheating are all increasing. We appear to be becoming a cheating society.

Even worse, people seem less ashamed of such petty thievery. Towels from motel chains are openly used in some homes. Pilfered office supplies often are not hidden. Students freely admit stealing exam answers: as one student said to the class before the professor arrived, "Remember, united we pass; divided I fail."

That attitude is partly explained by the perverted ethical notion that if you don't obviously hurt anyone personally, stealing is not so wrong. And because governments, banks, corporations, and stores are impersonal money-makers, people think they can easily absorb any losses. The man who'd be horrified at the idea of snatching an old woman's purse blithely steals an equivalent amount from his employer by padding his expense account. The woman who'd never dream of swiping a piece of her friend's silverware may wordlessly accept the money she's "long-changed" in a department store.

Our main case ("CDs for Tom and Thomas") is a good example of such rationalization. A young man takes advantage of an introductory "free CD" offer by submitting a variety of similar names, each time receiving a number of free CDs, something all his friends are doing without thinking twice. It's a good case to get you and the class into the ethics of petty theft of the kind that many people of all ages—including Christians—practice today.

People often justify such actions by arguing that "we're just getting back a little of our own." Stories of how stores overcharge, experiences of being short-changed, awareness of government waste, tales of corporate chicanery all make people feel they're only cheating cheaters and stealing from greater thieves. That makes our petty stealing seem almost good by comparison.

You can use today's case to teach some clear-cut, biblical truths:

- First, the idea that nobody's hurt by small thefts is a complete deception. The cheater cheats himself. The stealer steals from herself. The deepest hurt is to one's self. Every time we steal something from someone's locker, cheat on an exam, or lie on an income tax return, we take what God has *not* given. We lose the ability to thankfully receive God's gifts and then use them, enjoy them, and share them before the Lord.

- Second, when we steal, we hurt others. We sin against our neighbor. Our little theft might be passed on through increased prices and spread out so that it seems to do little harm. But it does do harm. It takes what belongs to others. To steal a penny from our neighbor is no less theft than stealing one hundred dollars. It's just easier to excuse.

■ Third, even petty thievery disrupts the ethical harmony of our lives, making us less liable to do good to our neighbor and less obedient to God. When we take another's possessions, we reject the principle of stewardship. Being a steward means recognizing that our goods, our time, our talents—all we have—belong to God. They're given into our care. We're responsible to God for their proper use. Stewardship emphasizes not the *possession of property* but its *use*. The rich farmer in Jesus' parable is condemned as a fool (Luke 12:15-21). His foolishness lies not in his thrift but in his response to having more grain than he needed: instead of considering how he might use it, he thought only of how he could store it. It was given to him to use, not to keep; so he quickly lost it all.

Being good stewards extends to our money as well. It makes us look twice at gambling, which places the money God has given us at high risk, encourages greed, and hurts far too many who practice it. Our alternate case ("Slots or Not") takes a look at gambling that's sponsored by government in both Canada and the States to raise money for good causes such as education and health care. Before your students reach the age where they can play the slots or buy a lottery ticket, they need to think about the issues and the consequences involved.

Our attitude toward the things that God has given us is at the heart of today's session. It's wrong to value goods as if they themselves were worth anything. They're given to us by God to use—for ourselves and our families certainly, but also for other people. That's the positive side of the eighth commandment—"That I do whatever I can for my neighbor's good, that I treat others as I would like them to treat me, and that I work faithfully so that I may share with those in need (Heidelberg Catechism, Q&A 111).

—HAS

LEADING THE SESSION

1 Presentations: The Many Faces of Theft
Materials: Resource Page: "Eighth Commandment" (one copy per student, p. 143), newsprint, marker

Use the first part of today's session to expand students' notions of what is meant by stealing or theft. Hand out one copy of the resource page to each student, and ask someone to read the eighth commandment and Q&A 110. Ask students to find four categories of "theft" mentioned by the Heidelberg Catechism:

■ outright theft and robbery (punishable by law)

■ cheating and swindling our neighbor

■ greed (wanting and taking more than we need)

■ squandering (wasting) of things given to us by God

Divide into groups of two to four students each. Assign one of the four categories of theft listed above to each group. Each group should dramatize (act out or pantomime) two examples of theft in the category they've been assigned. They have five minutes to plan their presentations.

TIP
Hey, this is supposed to be fun! Tell your small groups to loosen up and add some humor to their presentations. By the way, if you don't have enough students (at least eight) for the four categories, have the teams do just one presentation but in two different categories (or see the option below, which will work even if you're down to two or three students total.)

89

After five minutes, call time and start the presentations. Applaud each one, no matter how it turned out. When you finish with a category, ask the entire group for additional examples within that category. Remember, the idea is to expand our notion of what constitutes "stealing." Here are a few possibilities (you may want to list your examples on newsprint or on your board):

Outright theft

- taking something from someone's locker
- robbing a bank, gas station, or someone's piggy bank
- sneaking into a movie or game without a ticket
- goofing off at work or helping yourself to "free samples" while working
- ruining someone else's property (vandalism)
- returning something that you broke to the store for credit

Cheating and swindling our neighbors

- copying from a neighbor's test or paper
- plagiarism
- copying copyrighted material, such as a video or CD
- selling something as "good" that you know is defective
- charging someone far too much for something
- taking a good grade for a group project at school without doing any of the work
- asking to "borrow" something but having no intention of returning it

Greed

- gambling
- spending all your money on yourself
- never doing anything for someone else, just for yourself
- being satisfied with nothing less than the most expensive clothes
- not being a team player
- living as if we North Americans are entitled to more than anyone else

Waste

- dumping half your lunch at school
- wasting electricity, heat, water
- refusing to recycle

- driving at high speeds

- spending hours every day playing video games or watching TV

- not using your God-given talents

Conclude by saying something like this: **Now that we've had a look at what the commandment says we *should not* do, what do you think the commandment requires that we *should* do?** Listen to suggestions, then ask someone to read Matthew 7:12 and/or Q&A 111 from the resource page as a summary of the positive requirements of the commandment.

---

option: alternative to opening dramatizations

Begin by giving everyone a notecard and a pen. Ask each person to list two or three examples of things they've heard about or witnessed that they would consider some form of stealing or theft. Have them read their examples as you (or another student) make a master list on newsprint. Then read Q&A 110, note the four categories of theft, and classify the examples the students gave. If you wish, add other examples in each category (see list in step l). Conclude with the positive side of the commandment and Q&A 111.

2 Bible Study:
The Rich Fool, Then and Now
Materials: Resource Page: "Eighth Commandment," pens

Ask for a volunteer to read "The Parable of the Rich Fool" (side 2). Then give everyone five minutes to use their imaginations to fill in the blanks in "The Parable of the Rich Kid," a contemporary version of the parable. Explain that there are no "right answers"—you're looking for lots of variety and imagination in the responses.

After five minutes, call time and have fun sampling the contemporary parables. You can do this in different ways.

- If your class is very small, have students read all the way through their stories, or alternate students after a paragraph or so.

- For a larger class, go around the circle, having a different student read his or her response for each blank. Repeat the procedure, starting with another student, for a whole different story.

- Simply work your way through the story, calling on two or three students to give their response for each blank.

TIP

If students don't mention some of the above, you could read them the item and ask them to place it in one of the four categories.

TIP

You may want to give students the choice of working with a partner or two on this activity.

Remember to be sensitive to students who may feel (with good reason) that they've been short-changed when it comes to posses-sions, as least com-pared with some of their friends or class-mates. Acknowledge that we don't all have "tons of stuff," like the rich kid in our parables; howev-er, we don't have to be rich to get caught up in the possession game. The person to whom Jesus addressed this para-ble was probably a person of modest means who hoped to improve his lot in life by beating his brother's claim to an inheritance. Jesus reminded him and all of us—rich and poor—to be on our guard against all kinds of greed.

TIP

You may want to share this little say-ing from Andrew Kuyvenhoven: "Worship God, love people, use things." If we get these mixed up ("love things, use people"), we're in big trouble!

After the readings, ask questions along these lines:

■ **At the beginning of today's session, we looked at a bunch of ways to break the eighth commandment. Was the rich man guilty of any of these?** Note his greed for more things but also his waste of resources by storing them, not using them.

■ **What do you suppose the rich man should have done with at least some of his resources?**

■ **What questions about your own possessions does this parable raise in your mind?** Allow time for students to reflect a little before answering. Encourage honesty by sharing questions the parable raises in your mind about your own use of posses-sions.

■ **What important principle about our possessions can you find in Psalm 24:1 (resource page)?** Emphasize that everything we have belongs to God. All the "stuff" we have is on loan from God, who is the real owner of the whole business.

option: skit

Instead of the "fill-in-the-blank" activity, have students act out the parable. Characters could include the rich person, a narrator (to spin out the story and describe what's happening), the rich man's wife and friends, a variety of inanimate objects (such as crops, goods, and barns) and barn wreckers and builders. The idea is to embellish the original story and have fun doing so. To save time, play the part of the narrator yourself and appoint others to the various roles. While this works best with large classes, you can adapt it to smaller groups by having students take multiple roles.

3 **Case Study:
CDs for Tom and Thomas**
Materials: Resource Page: "Eighth Commandment," Case Study Card: "CDs for Tom and Thomas" (or alternate: "Slots or Not?"), newsprint, markers

To introduce today's case, you could take an informal poll of our students, asking how many get their CDs mostly from local stores, how many through the mail, how many from friends or over the Internet. Comment that today's case centers on what has been a very common way of obtaining CDs: through "introductory offers" made by companies through the mail. Read the case "CDs for Tom and Thomas" to the class. (For alternate case, see option on page 94.)

Divide into small groups of two to four students each. Give each group a sheet of newsprint and a marker. Ask half of the groups to list reasons from the case (and their own minds) why it would be OK for Tom to continue obtaining free CDs under variations of his own name. Ask the other half to list reasons from the case (and their own minds) why it would not be OK for Tom to do this. Allow about five minutes to complete this task.

activity adaptation

If you or your students are weary of working in groups, lead the entire class in this discussion. Enlist the help of a student to jot down reasons (pro and con) on two sheets of newsprint you've posted on the classroom wall.

After five minutes or so, review what the teams wrote. Sample responses follow:

Reasons for Getting Free CDs

- Lots of kids do it and think nothing of it.

- Lots of parents do similar things (multiple purchase of limited quantity items in grocery stores, for example).

- Companies know and expect people to do this—it's all covered by their marketing budgets.

- Companies would stop if they weren't making money.

- Companies make enough off "shipping and handling" to cover any losses from people who sign up more than once for free CDs.

- This isn't stealing—it's just being a smart consumer.

Reasons Against Getting Free CDs

- Tom and his friends are clearly violating the "one-to-a-customer" rule of the offer.

- This is a form of "cheating and swindling" that the Bible and the Catechism warn about. Tom is, in effect, taking money that rightly belongs to the company.

- The loss the company incurs may be passed along to other customers; in effect, Tom's action also takes money from other customers who have to pay more for their CDs.

- A signature is a form of saying, "This is true." Tom and his friends are lying by using a false signature.

- Though the amount of money involved may be small, the Bible says that if we're dishonest in small matters, we'll be dishonest in bigger matters too.

When you've worked through all the reasons, pass out slips of paper and ask students to write yes or no to indicate their approval or disapproval of what Tom is doing. Collect the votes and announce the results.

Ask, **Based on what the case says, what do you think Tom decided to do?** You can tell them that, in fact, Tom did mail the letter, telling himself that when he got out of college and made more money, he would stop taking advantage of "introductory" offers.

TIP
This is a "teaching" case where (we think) there is a clear moral *ought*. Tom ought not to do what he is doing. Though widely practiced, even by Christians, it is a form of theft. You don't want to be dogmatic about it, but do communicate this to your students.

93

option: alternate case study: slots or not?

May Christians buy lottery tickets, knowing that much of the profit goes to good causes like education or the arts or health care? How about spending a carefully limited and small amount of money on the slots at a casino? Or how about spending a few bucks on a raffle for a new car sponsored by a local organization trying to raise money for a charity? These are questions your students will have to answer for themselves sometime soon. The case, "Slots or Not?" can lay the groundwork for their decision.

You may want to begin by raising questions such as the above. Then read the case and divide into small groups of three to five students each. Ask the groups to decide what Cathy should do and why. Give them about fifteen minutes to come to a conclusion and to jot it down, along with supporting reasons, on newsprint. Encourage them to use their own reasons as well as the reasons given in the case. And, of course, they can bring in the material on the resource page as well.

After fifteen minutes, ask the groups to display their newsprint summary and report. In the event that the students in a single group can't reach a consensus on what Cathy should do, they may submit a "majority" and "minority" report, if they wish to do so. Sample responses follow:

Reasons Cathy should vote yes:

- Playing the slots is strictly voluntary. Persons who don't believe it's right don't have to do it.

- Proceeds go to the general budget, which includes some very good causes, such as education and health care. For the most part, profits are put to good use in serving the public.

- The slots will help lower the income tax for everyone, including persons who are poor.

- Addiction to gambling affects only a small minority of players. Why deprive the majority of some harmless fun?

- Christians don't hesitate to risk their money in other ventures like the stock market, where they can also lose everything.

- Christians shouldn't impose their standards on society as a whole.

Reasons Cathy should vote no:

- Playing the slots (in fact, gambling of any kind) appeals to our greed— it's a quick and painless way to get rich.

- Far from being harmless, gambling "sucks money out of the poor and most vulnerable." We steal from the poor when we gamble.

- The end (helping to pay for education) does not justify the means (gambling).

- Addiction to gambling is a growing social (and personal) problem that Christians should be addressing, not contributing to.

- Our money belongs to God (Ps. 24:1). When we gamble, we waste it by betting against odds overwhelmingly stacked against us.

- Gambling—attempting to get rich quick—is a way of saying we don't trust God to provide for all our needs.

- Gambling, especially in casinos, often brings with it a host of social problems, including increased crime and prostitution.

After your discussion, you may want to hand out paper ballots and have individuals vote yes (for the proposal) or no (against it). You can tell them that Cathy, along with a majority in the rest of her town and province, voted against the slots, as did a number of other regions throughout the province. However, some two years after the vote, the provincial government has not removed a single slot machine from any of these areas, and the issue has been dropped for lack of interest. At the date of this printing, slots are still used throughout Alberta. Since the slots hold down taxes, there's no political will to reverse this policy.

As a way of summarizing the issue, you could read the following statement about gambling adopted by the synod of the Christian Reformed Church:

> Pastors and church councils are urged to expose all destructive influences on people's lives that seek to trivialize or render irrelevant the providence of God. They must also caution against the impact of materialism, take decisive action to combat the evil of gambling, and minister compassionately to those addicted to or victimized by lotteries.
>
> —From *Doctrinal and Ethical Decisions of the Christian Reformed Church in North America*

Synod's full report also deplored the growing dependence of governments (city, regional, and national) on gambling revenues to do their job. The report raises the question of how the agencies that are supposed to regulate gambling are themselves the biggest stake-holders!

4 Closing:
Commitment and Guided Prayer
Materials: Resource Page: "Eighth Commandment," pens

We suggest concluding with an emphasis on the positive side of the commandment. Ask someone to read Q&A 111 once more. Remind the group of how much God has given each of us—all of it on loan from God. Everything we have belongs to God.

Invite everyone to think of one specific way he or she could "share with those in need," something they are willing to do during the next week or two. For example, they might give up buying a CD or going to a movie, giving the money saved to a charitable organization that helps the poor. Ask them to write their commitment next to Q&A 111 on the resource page. This is personal information, not for sharing.

Conclude with a time of guided prayer, pausing for students to pray silently after phrases like the following:

- **Dear God, thank you for all that you have given to us on loan, especially for . . .**

- **Please forgive those times that I've been guilty of stealing from others, of cheating or swindling, of greed, of wasting your gifts. Especially, dear God, forgive me for . . .**

- **Please make me generous in sharing with others what you've given to me. Especially, dear God, help me keep my commitment to . . . Amen.**

the ninth commandment

SESSION FOCUS

The ninth commandment forbids all forms of lying; it requires us to love the truth and tell it in a loving way.

SCRIPTURE

Exodus 20:16; Proverbs 12:22; Colossians 3:9; Ephesians 4:15; John 14:6, 16-17; Acts 4:32-5:11

SESSION GOALS

- to give at least three reasons why Christians ought not to lie

- to identify exceptions to the ninth commandment

- to apply this commandment to a case study

- to commit to being truthful in a specific area of our lives when we might be tempted to lie

SESSION AT A GLANCE

Learning Activity	Materials	Time
1. *Survey: The Lies We Tell.* We get a sense of the pervasiveness of lying by ranking a variety of untruths from most offensive to least offensive.	Resource Page: "Ninth Commandment" (one copy per student, p. 147), pens	10 minutes
2. *Bible Study: Why God Hates Lying.* We read the story of Ananias and Sapphira and other passages, then compile a list of reasons why God is so opposed to lying.	Resource Page: "Ninth Commandment"	15-20 minutes
3. *Case Study: Just Tell Me What You Know.* Small groups write advice to the main character in this case, basing the advice on biblical principles and projecting consequences for those involved. (Alternate case and discussion approach provided.)	Resource Page: "Ninth Commandment," Case Study Card: "Just Tell Me What You Know" (or alternate: "Cement Is Hard"), newsprint, markers	20 minutes
4. *Resolution: To Tell the Truth.* We write personal statements that remind us to tell the truth in relationships and settings where we might be tempted to lie.	Notecards, pens	5 minutes

SESSION BACKGROUND

False testimony: the term evokes a courtroom scene. An innocent victim sits, hopeless and frustrated, broken by the perjury of a false witness. (Remember the scene in *To Kill a Mockingbird* or Jezebel's treatment of Naboth.) How do we cope with lying? When deceit is rife, whom can we trust?

People have always lied, from Cain's disclaimer of any knowledge of his murdered brother's whereabouts to a recent U.S. president's denial of an affair with an intern. Lying eats like an acid pool at society's foundation pillars, creating suspicion, skepticism, and distrust, and alienating people from one another. But in recent years bland disregard for truth and a flood of public and private falsehoods has been more like a spring storm tearing away the sandy foundation of a house on the shore. Pervasive mistrust of politicians' promises, skepticism about news reports, and cynicism about official statements that so commonly slant the truth or present it partially have become common.

In all its forms, from silence to slander, from polite half-truths to mean twisting of words, the lie drives people apart from each other and from God. Lying destroys. It destroys communication, it destroys the value of talking, it destroys my neighbor's good name, it even destroys my integrity.

In contrast to all this, Christians must love the truth, seek it out, reverence it, protect and preserve it, and tell it. Yet even truth-telling stands under the one ethical absolute of love to God and neighbor. Christians must "tell the truth in love" (Eph. 4:15).

Love is the test of full truthfulness. Truth-telling, like Sabbath-keeping, should be intended to help and heal, should be meant for our neighbor's good. As the Catechism says in Answer 112, "I should do what I can to guard and advance my neighbor's good name."

Love keeps us from telling brutal truths that speak an unkind, unhelpful word: "You'll never play the piano well. Why waste your time?" or "Josh, I'd rather spend an evening picking lint off my socks than go out with you." Love keeps us from using truth to destroy, to defame, to cut someone down. On rare occasions love for neighbor allows us to withhold the truth or even say a word contrary to fact. When the Gestapo was rounding up the Jews in Europe to effect the "final solution," some Christians hid them and boldly lied to save them. In that circumstance, a lie was the only right choice. Sometimes it is our moral obligation not to tell—to give partial, incomplete, or even false information. But at the same time, we must love the truth and work for an improved situation in which the full truth can be told.

The classic case about lying to spare the lives of innocent Jews is an exception. In most circumstances we are obligated to tell the truth. Truth keeps us honest, keeps us from flattery, from saying things only to please others: "You're looking younger every day, Grandma. Honest!" Truth keeps us from those little "white lies" that are so easily and conveniently told: "I'm late because I got caught in traffic." "I can't go out with you because I have to babysit." "He's not available to answer the phone right now." As Joy Davidman says in *Smoke on the Mountain,* most white lies are told out of laziness or cowardice, not out of concern for others.

Again and again, the Word of God reminds us to tell the truth. Our lying allies us with the devil, the father of lies who deceived and tempted our first parents. God is truth. God's Word is truth. God's Spirit, who lives in us, is the Spirit of truth (John 14:16-17). We who bear Christ's name are his witnesses, committed to speaking the truth in him (Rom. 9:1).

Both of our cases today take students into that difficult area of knowing when—or when not—to tell a truth that is bound to get someone else in big trouble. The main case ("To Tell or Not to Tell") deals with honesty in a school setting. The alternate case ("Cement Is Hard") deals with a summer job situation. Blowing the whistle on others is not a popular thing to do, especially for teens, who often place a high value on approval of others. There are times when telling is a moral necessity, times when it may be appropriate, and times when it may be unnecessary and inappropriate. Sorting out the differences is what today's cases are about. At the very least, both cases demonstrate that truth-telling can be painfully difficult.

The ninth commandment requires love for truth and truth in love. In Christian ethics, truth and love are joined not in forced union but as natural mates. For the children of God's love are born of God's truth; those who love God have *become* truth and speak the truth in Christ.

—HAS

LEADING THE SESSION

1 Survey: The Lies We Tell

Materials: Resource Page: "Ninth Commandment" (one copy per student, p. 147), pens

Distribute copies of the resource page for each student, and ask someone to read the ninth commandment. Challenge students to come up with a popular rephrasing of that commandment ("Don't lie!" or "Tell the truth!").

Then give students five minutes to complete the survey on the resource page, ranking a variety of lies from "most offensive" to "least offensive." Note that they may add their own examples and rank those as well. This exercise should be done quickly. The intent of the survey is not to arrive at some correct "priority" of various types of lying but mainly to remind students of the prevalence of lying in our society.

After five minutes, sample the top three and bottom three responses from the class. Ask for reasons for their ranking. See if you and the class can isolate some factors that make some lies more serious than others. For example, some lies may be told maliciously, with intent to harm others, whereas other lies may be told to avoid hurting someone's feelings. In other words, our motive may affect the seriousness of a lie. Some lies have much more serious consequences than others. And some lies may affect more people than other lies.

Conclude by commenting that lying of all sorts is so common that we've grown used to it and even expect it. The ninth commandment, of all the commandments, is often taken very lightly. Lying is probably the least sensitive moral area, and untruthfulness causes the least concern.

TIP
If you wish, give students the choice of working with a partner on this activity.

99

2 Bible Study: Why God Hates Lying
Materials: Resource Page: "Ninth Commandment"

Comment that God's attitude toward lying contrasts sharply with that of many people today. Ask for a volunteer to read the short passages listed under "More on the Ninth Commandment."

Perhaps nowhere in the Bible is God's attitude toward lying shown more clearly and shockingly than in the story of Ananias and Sapphira. Ask students to imagine that they are eyewitnesses to what happened, as you read the passage aloud from the resource page.

When you come to the end of the passage, ask students to fill in the blank space with words that describe how the whole church could have felt about the incident. After a minute or two, ask for several volunteers to share their response. Wrap up by telling the class how Eugene Peterson, author of the paraphrase *The Message*, interpreted the remainder of this verse: **"By this time the whole church and, in fact, everyone who heard of these things . . . had healthy respect for God. They knew God was not to be trifled with."**

Continue by asking questions like the following:

■ **Why do you suppose God is so opposed to lying?** Please ask students to draw on their own experiences as well as the Bible passages listed on the resource page.

100

Emphasize that God prohibits lying because it is so damaging to those who tell the lie as well as those to whom the lie is told. In addition, we are followers of Jesus Christ, who is the truth (John 14:6). And we have the Spirit of truth within us (John 14:16-17). Please see the session background for additional reasons.

■ **Agree or disagree with this statement: "We should always tell the truth, the whole truth, no matter what the consequences. There is simply no time when any lie is excusable."** Listen to student responses and summarize by affirming that the Bible means exactly what it says—"Do not lie to one another." Lying is punished. It causes no end of trouble. But, under certain rare circumstances, we may lie if telling the truth causes serious harm to life, thereby violating the command to love our neighbors. Let students give some examples (a lie told in wartime; a lie told to protect one's own life or the lives of others; a lie told by a national leader, denying he has spies operating in a country when he knows full well they are). Remind students of the "love within law" principle they learned earlier in this course. The ninth commandment, like the others, needs to be seen in the context of love.

■ **What are some examples of times when the "law of love" might keep us from telling the full and candid truth because it might be unkind or damaging to someone?** Affirm the need for truth-telling in our communications with each other. But note that love for others prevents us from being brutally honest in certain situations. See the Session Background for examples.

Conclude the step by asking someone to read Q&A 112 to the class.

3 Case Study:
Just Tell Me What You Know
Materials: Resource Page: "Ninth Commandment," Case Study Card: "Just Tell Me What You Know" (or alternate: "Cement Is Hard"), newsprint, markers

To introduce the case, ask: **How many of you have been in a situation where you've been asked to reveal information about someone or something to a parent or teacher?** Comment that it can be really tough to be in a situation where you're not sure whether you should tell what you know or remain silent. On the one hand we don't want others to think we're self-righteous tattletales, but on the other hand we really want to be truthful and honest. That's the dilemma facing Tim in our case study. Read it aloud to the class. (For alternate case, see option on p. 103.)

To discuss this case, we suggest forming small groups of two to four students each who act as "friends of Tim." The groups are to imagine that Tim has come to them for advice about what to do in this situation. They are talking about what to tell him. The following are among the questions the friends should discuss before dispensing advice (put these on newsprint or on your board for easy reference):

■ **What biblical principles should Tim be thinking about? Is there any evidence that he's aware of these principles?**

■ **What are the possible consequences of telling (for Tim and for the suspects)? Of not telling?**

101

Have the groups jot down (on newsprint) a short version of what they advise Tim to do and why. Allow up to fifteen minutes for the groups to work.

Before the groups report, you may want to review the two questions above. On the question of **biblical principles,** the fact that Tim is wondering what to do shows some awareness of the principle of truthfulness. Telling the truth matters to Tim. If it didn't, the lie would be much easier for him to tell. Also, the principle of love for neighbor can be seen in Tim's concern that Bill and Kevin might be innocent and therefore suffer needlessly. Tim also is concerned that his telling might prevent Bill and Kevin from graduating. He does not seem to show any concern for the well-being of the school community as a whole, as Mr. Ortega clearly does. His own well-being—what others will think of him and do to him—seems to be foremost in his mind.

On the issue of **possible consequences,** Tim runs the risk of others finding out if he tells, with the resulting social stigma and possible retaliation from Bill and Kevin. In addition, he may come to see himself as someone who tells on others. And because he doesn't have conclusive proof of Bill and Kevin's guilt, he runs the risk of putting innocent people through a lot of unnecessary trouble. If they are guilty, telling on them could cause them not to graduate, a serious result for what was intended only as a prank. On the other hand, not telling could result in a guilty conscience. It could let the guilty go free, and perhaps encourage Bill and Kevin—as well as others—to try similar stunts.

activity adaptation

If time is short, skip discussing the two questions as described above and go directly to the small group reports. Watch for and point out places where small groups did bring in biblical principles and consequences.

After the preliminary discussion, call on the groups of "friends" to share their advice to Tim. Since Tim has been asked very directly by Mr. Ortega if he knows anything about the case, he is under a very strong obligation to tell what he does know—unless he has a very good reason for not doing so. A central consideration may be Tim's lack of certainty about Bill and Kevin's involvement—is it loving and kind of him to report something that could get innocent people in trouble? However, Tim can get around this issue, if he wishes, by clearly telling the principal that his information is based only on what he heard from his friends, not on direct proof of any kind.

After the presentations, you can tell the class that Tim did explain to the principal the two incidents he knew about, noting his lack of direct proof and begging the principal not to tell Bill and Kevin or anyone else about his supplying the information. Bill and Kevin were called in and eventually admitted that they had glued the locks and damaged the building. They had to pay for all the repairs—over $1,000—and were allowed to graduate.

option: alternate to small groups

Instead of the small group approach above, you could have students individually write Tim a short letter of advice, suggesting what he ought to do and why. Remind students to think about biblical principles and to project consequences when they are writing their advice (or hold a preliminary discussion with the whole class about this). Have all students read their letters, then call attention to differences in the advice that students wrote. Ask if anyone would change his or her advice, based on what others said. Then reveal the way the case actually ended.

option: alternate case study: cement is hard

Introduce the case by asking students if they've ever encountered any issues involving the ninth commandment in their part-time job experiences. Have they ever been asked to do something on the job that they thought was less than honest or unfair to the customer? Examples, if any, can be told without identifying the employer. You may want to share a story from your own work experience.

Read the case to the class. As in the main case, you could divide into small groups of "friends of Jim" offering advice—backed up by reasons. Or discuss with the entire class, using questions like these:

- **If Jim remains silent, is that a form of lying? Why or why not?**

- **How does the "love for neighbor" principle enter this case?** The people who are paying for the sidewalk to be installed are getting less for their money than what they've been told to expect. They are being cheated. Concern for them could be a motivation for reporting the incident. On the other hand, what about concern for his employer, who would perhaps have to pay fines and who would almost certainly raise his prices to future customers? What about his dad, who was a good friend of Jim's employer—would it be fair to end their friendship over an issue like this?

- **What options are possible for Jim? Which option seems best to you? Why?** An interesting issue here is whether just quitting and finding another job is enough, or if telling the building inspector is also required. Talk about the consequences of each option, and try to reach a consensus on which option honors the truth and the "love your neighbor" principle that we learned about earlier in this course. Exactly how should Jim go about "speaking the truth in love," as Ephesians 4:15 asks us to do?

Conclude by telling the class that Jim talked to his dad about the situation. His dad listened and gave no advice, other than to say that he, the father, could not help with the college tuition and that the job Jim held paid very well. Jim said nothing more and worked on the sidewalk project for the rest of the summer. In retrospect, many years later, he believes he should have should have objected to the practice once more with the owner. Then, if the owner said he would continue the practice, either quit on principle, or quit and call the city building inspector with information about the owner's practice.

TIP

It doesn't hurt to acknowledge here that truth-telling is a commandment that most of us find very hard to keep. The Bible says that no one can tame the tongue. We are all in need of God's grace and God's forgiveness. You may want to include a time of silent prayer for forgiveness and guidance.

4 Resolution: To Tell the Truth

Materials: notecards, pens

Distribute notecards and ask students to think about a relationship or setting with parents or teachers or friends or employers in which they might be tempted to lie. Ask them to write a private resolution to "speak the truth in love" in that specific relationship or setting. If they wish, they may include a Bible text from the resource page or elsewhere as part of their resolution. Ask them to take the notecard home with them, perhaps tucking it in their Bibles at home as their personal reminder to tell the truth in this situation.

the tenth commandment

SESSION FOCUS

The tenth commandment forbids us to covet our neighbor's possessions; it requires us to be content, finding our worth not in our belongings but in belonging to Jesus Christ.

SCRIPTURE

Exodus 20:17; 1 Kings 21; 2 Corinthians 11:24-29; Philippians 4:12-13

SESSION GOALS

- to give examples of things we may be tempted to covet
- to explain what we can learn about coveting and contentment from the example of Ahab and Paul
- to apply the tenth commandment to a case study about coveting
- to express gratitude for the many ways God has blessed us

SESSION AT A GLANCE

Learning Activity	Materials	Time
1. Activity: *Updating the Commandment.* We work in pairs to update the tenth commandment in terms of things we might be tempted to covet.	Resource Page: "Tenth Commandment" (one copy per student, p. 151), pens, newsprint, markers, masking tape	10-15 minutes
2. Bible Study: *Coveting Versus Contentment.* We discuss the story of Ahab's coveting Naboth's vineyard, then look at Paul's contentment in all circumstances.	Resource Page: "Tenth Commandment"	20 minutes
3. Case Study: *Marcy's Moment.* Small groups write an ending to a case involving coveting of a friend's relationship with a guy at school. (Alternate case and discussion approach provided.)	Resource Page: "Tenth Commandment," Case Study Card: "Marcy's Moment" (or alternate case: "A Car to Covet")	20 minutes
4. Prayer: *Gratitude for God's Gifts.* We think of one thing God has given us for which we are very grateful, then participate in a litany of thanks.	None needed	5 minutes

105

SESSION BACKGROUND

Coveting is an ardent craving for what belongs to someone else. Think of it, if you will, as a kind of mental theft, a deep longing for another's possessions. What kind of possessions? The tenth commandment gets right down to specifics: "You shall not covet your neighbor's house . . . wife . . . manservant or maidservant . . . ox or donkey, or anything that belongs to your neighbor." Something of a curious list, if you stop to think of it—a wife included as a possession. You may prefer the Deuteronomic version, which at least places wife before house and servants.

Still the message is clear: coveting is wrong. We may not selfishly and excessively desire possessions, especially not those that belong to another person. Please note that the commandment is not talking about satisfying our normal, God-implanted needs for things like food and drink, shelter, clothing, love, and dignity; rather, it addresses excessive wants and desires that go far beyond needs. It addresses selfishly wanting for ourselves what belongs to others. These are needs that have become desires without proper limits.

The commandment speaks of coveting the *neighbor's* possessions. That's because in Bible times one became aware of and lusted for a handsomer or prettier spouse, a bigger house, a better cook, a stronger ox, a more willing donkey, by seeing another person who had these. Think, for example, of Ahab's coveting Naboth's vineyard, a story your students discuss in today's session. Glancing out of his palace window, Ahab sees his neighbor's prime piece of property and is immediately seized by a desire to own it and transform it into a vegetable garden. Never mind that he is king of the land and already has far more of everything than he'll ever need. Turned down by Naboth, he takes to his bed in a royal sulk, refusing even to eat. Then, urged on by his wife, he agrees to Naboth's murder, an act that outrages the Lord and brings disaster on the king and his household.

Like Ahab, we also are capable of casting envious glances at our neighbors. In our main case ("Marcy's Moment"), a teen covets the friendship of a young man who has been dating someone else. The alternate case ("A Car to Covet") features a teen who must decide just how badly he wants a new set of wheels like those driven by his friends.

We covet by looking at our neighbor's possessions and wanting them for ourselves. But our coveting is fueled by a relentless barrage of advertisements that focus on getting more and more things. In newspapers and magazines, on TV and the Internet, we see a daily cornucopia of attractive possessions—handsome men and beautiful women (wives), superb homes (houses), computers and cell phones (servants), new machines of every description (oxen) and new cars and SUVs (donkeys). We're invited to covet, urged to become discontented with what we have, to long for more, better, faster, more expensive, and more comfortable belongings.

It is easy for us to be possessed by things, to turn our hearts toward possessions and away from God.

In contrast, Paul says he's learned "the secret of being content in any and every situation, whether well fed or hungry, whether living in plenty or in want" (Phil. 4:12). Paul learned to be satisfied with what God gives. In the next verse, he says, "I can do everything through him who gives me strength." Paul was no longer anxious about possessions because his attention was fixed on God. He found his contentment in actively and busily serving God.

Coveting can be an insidious bondage. Things rule us. The tenth commandment tells us to be free of that tyranny; it warns us not to covet but also points us toward being content in Jesus Christ. Contentment in Christ is the positive side, the moral *ought* of the tenth commandment. True contentment lies not so much in possessing as in being possessed. It lies in knowing that we are Christ's prized possessions. It comes from believing that "I am not my own but belong—body and soul, in life and in death—to my faithful Savior Jesus Christ" (Heidelberg Catechism, Q&A 1).

Because we belong to Jesus, we have more worth than all the world's belongings can give us.

—HAS

LEADING THE SESSION

1 Activity: Updating the Commandment

Materials: Resource Page: "Tenth Commandment" (one copy per student, p. 151), pens, newsprint, markers, masking tape

Begin by asking someone to read the tenth commandment from the resource page. Ask, **What does it mean to covet?** Listen to responses, then summarize: **Coveting is a strong craving or desire for something that belongs to someone else.** Take a moment to differentiate between coveting and legitimate need and desire. Desire, zeal, or drive for the right things is not coveting (see 1 Cor. 14:1, for example). Coveting implies an obsession, a strong desire for something that doesn't rightfully belong to us.

Divide the class into pairs and give each pair a marker and a sheet of newsprint. Ask each pair to update the tenth commandment (see Ex. 20:17, resource sheet). The pairs should write out their version of the commandment, substituting things *they* might be tempted to covet (instead of a neighbor's house, wife, servants, and so on).

Allow about five minutes for the pairs to finish. Then have the pairs tape their rewrites to the wall (or otherwise display them) and read them aloud.

Conclude by asking questions like these:

■ **What kind of pressure, if any, do you feel to "keep up" with the stuff your friends have—stuff like the items we've listed in our rewrites of the tenth commandment?** Talk about the way our society encourages and almost pushes us into coveting. Everywhere we turn, it seems, we are urged to buy the latest and the biggest, to keep up with our neighbors, to scorn last year's styles, to go along with the latest trends, to accumulate (see also Session Background).

■ **How does coveting hurt us?** Coveting affects our attitude and makes us dissatisfied with what we have, never content. It also poisons our relationship with those persons we envy.

■ **What ultimately makes us discontented with what God has given us?** Emphasize that, despite all the pressures around us to covet, we really don't have any

TIP
There's no need to try to match each item in the commandment with a contemporary item. Simply have students rewrite the commandment in terms of things that they would be tempted to covet.

TIP
You may want to give an example of something you've personally coveted at some time in your life, and tell how you dealt with the situation.

excuses. Ultimately, coveting comes down to an attitude of the heart, a sinful mind-set that's deep inside every fallen human being.

---

option: alternate opening

Bring a number of magazine or newspaper advertisements that push readers in the general direction of coveting, of outdoing the neighbor, of not being content with what they have. Read the tenth commandment with the class, then distribute the ads and talk about pressures our society places on people to be discontented with what they have. If time permits, distribute large sheets of paper and markers. Have pairs pretend to be marketers to a teen audience and create an ad that uses coveting as a device to sell a product to teens.

TIP

If you have more than eight students, ask those not reading to act as an impromptu audience, booing the villain, cheering the hero, and adding other sound effects as they think appropriate. If you have fewer than eight students, use one narrator and one scoundrel, and have students read multiple parts (or simply read the passage directly from the Bible as narrative instead of reader's theater.

2 Bible Study: Coveting Versus Contentment
Materials: Resource Page: "Tenth Commandment"

Our Bible study today offers a study in contrasts: Ahab, who has everything but covets even more, and Paul, who has next to nothing but is content.

Begin by quickly assigning roles for the reader's theater version of 1 Kings 21: One Man's Envy (resource page). You'll need readers for

- two narrators
- King Ahab
- Jezebel
- two scoundrels
- the Lord
- Elijah

Give students a moment to look at their lines and ask about pronunciation, if necessary. Ask them to read with expression, adding gestures and movement if they wish.

Afterward, discuss the questions that are printed on the resource sheet:

- **How would you classify Ahab's case of coveting: mild or severe? Why?** It should be apparent that Ahab has a severe case of the covets. He's angry and upset, he sulks, he goes to bed and refuses to eat. He's a king but he's acting like a little kid. Can students imagine the president or prime minister carrying on like this? (Maybe that's not a good question to ask!)

- **Imagine yourself as Ahab. You are defending your coveting and the action you took. What would you say?** Ask one or two of your talkers to give a short spiel or

108

spin from Ahab's point of view. It could go something like this: *Hey, I'm the king, right? I'm supposed to get my way all the time, every time, right? I really needed that dumb vineyard to grow my veggies—the king's got to stay healthy, you know. And I offered that skinflint Naboth a very good price. The nerve of him turning me down—me, the king of all Israel. Too bad he had to die, but he asked for it, that's for sure.*

■ **What can we learn about coveting from this story?** Quite a bit, actually. For instance, that having a whole lot of stuff doesn't make you immune to coveting; in fact, it may very well fuel it. And that coveting makes a person downright miserable and can drive him or her to extreme behavior. Even when the coveted object is finally obtained, it's often a letdown—or, in Ahab's case, a disaster.

■ **What can we learn about God from this story?** Coveting angers God (ask students why) and comes with a price. When we're guilty, God expects confession and humility. God is merciful as well as just. God will forgive us our coveting.

Switch to the second reading: "One Man's Contentment." Ask for a volunteer to read both passages to the class.

---

activity adaptation

Have an adult friend visit your class in the role of Paul (he can dress for the part, if he wishes) and paraphrase the two passages from Paul. Done well, this can have considerably more impact than just reading the passages aloud.

After the reading, discuss the questions that are printed on the resource page:

■ **If you were in Paul's shoes, what would you be tempted to covet?** A good night's sleep, a hot meal, a dry house, good company, a dull evening with his feet to the fire—all these things must have looked good to Paul.

■ **Unlike Ahab, who is discontented with much, Paul seems content with very little. What's his secret?** Paul says he is strengthened through Jesus Christ. In Christ, he finds everything he needs, and then some. Instead of being possessed by possessions, he is possessed by Jesus Christ.

■ **What helps you resist coveting and be content with what God has given you?** Invite students to share their ideas. Let them know you're not looking for some super scheme here, but just for down-to-earth ideas that help them stay close to God and content with God's gifts.

3 Case Study: Marcy's Moment

Resource Page: "Tenth Commandment," Case Study Card: "Marcy's Moment" (or alternate: "A Car to Covet")

Distribute today's case study card and read it to the class (see option on p. 111 for the alternate case).

To get students into the case, ask a couple of preliminary questions, along these lines:

- **Is Marcy guilty of coveting here or is she simply wanting to go out with a popular and likeable guy?** Have students refer to the case to support their responses.

- **What other commandment besides the tenth is involved in this case?** Truth-telling (the ninth commandment) is up for grabs here, as Marcy debates whether or not to tell Mitch about Laura's drinking incident. Is telling the truth about Laura "speaking the truth in love" or does it come closer to gossiping and slander and manipulation?

- **How do you feel about Marcy? Like her? Dislike her? Understand what she's going through?**

After questions like these, explain that you'd like students—working in groups of two or three—to think of an ending to "Marcy's Moment." Did Marcy tell Mitch about Laura or not? If not, did Mitch eventually find out, lose interest in Laura, and begin dating Marcy? If Marcy told, how did Mitch react? What happened to his relationship with Laura? Did things turn out the way Marcy wanted?

Explain that it's up to the small groups to present their story ending in an interesting way. One way, for example, would be to act out the ending they agree on. Another might be to have someone assume Marcy's or Bill's role and tell what happened in the car on the way home and later. Groups could also write an ending to the case and read it to the class.

Allow ten minutes for groups to prepare, then see what they came up with. After each presentation, ask the group why they ended the story as they did.

To conclude the activity, you can explain what really happened. Marcy did tell Mitch about Laura. He took it in, and, although he was shocked by it and condemned the behavior, he dated Laura again. Marcy also told Mitch about other things that Laura did later, things that didn't match Laura's Christian witness. Within two months, Mitch stopped dating Laura, but he didn't date Marcy either. Eventually, the group broke up as they went their different ways out of high school.

option: alternate case study: a car to covet

If you've taught *Decisions,* you may notice that this case has been updated from that course. You may want to use the same approach for the alternate case as for the main case: that is, begin with a couple of introductory questions, then have students act out or write an ending to the case.

Start by asking questions like these:

- How important is owning a car—a nice car—to someone in high school?

- Do you blame Ben for not wanting to drive the minivan at college? Why or why not?

- Is Ben guilty of coveting the Corolla? Why or why not?

- What other commandments—besides the tenth—could be involved in this case?

Ask students to work in small groups to present an ending to the case study (see directions in main case).

After their presentations, you can tell them that Ben decided he needed the money more than he needed the Corolla. He drove the minivan during his first year at college. To his surprise, his friends actually liked the beast! And Ben found that lots of other kids on campus drove vehicles even older and uglier than his. When the van died the following summer, Ben admitted he was sorry to see it go.

4 Prayer: Gratitude for God's Gifts
Materials: none needed

Comment that, in contrast to coveting, God wants us to have an "attitude of gratitude," to live in thankful appreciation of all God's good gifts.

Ask each person to think of one good gift of God for which he or she is especially thankful. After a moment, invite each person to say a sentence prayer of thanks. After each prayer, the entire group can respond with "Thank you, God, for your good gifts."

pressing on toward the goal

SESSION FOCUS

"Let us not become weary in doing good . . ." (Gal. 6:9).

SCRIPTURE

Matthew 5:1-12; 5:38-44; 22:34-40; Luke 9:23; John 14:15; 1 Corinthians 9:24-25; Galatians 5:22-23; 6:9-10; Philippians 3:12-14; 4:13; James 2:14-17

SESSION GOALS

- to restate the Ten Commandments positively in our own words as guidelines for Christian living

- to define "success" in Christian living not as getting ahead in this world but as living a life of joyful and loving obedience to Christ

- to be motivated to "press on toward the goal," despite our failures

SESSION AT A GLANCE

Learning Activity	Materials	Time
1. *Review: The Right Stuff.* Working in small groups, we state the commandments positively in our own words. We also look briefly at Christ's summary of the law and at several verses from the Sermon on the Mount.	Bibles, newsprint, markers, masking tape	15-20 minutes
2. *Reflection and Discussion: The Right Reasons.* We pick one of the commandments we restated that's particularly relevant to our lives right now, jot it on a notecard, and then jot down obstacles to keeping that commandment. Finally, we list our reasons for attempting to keep it.	Bibles, notecards (preferably 4" x 6"), pens	15 minutes
3. *Presentations: Press On!* Again working in small groups, we present (using drama or writing or art) one encouraging Bible passage to the class and add it to our notecards. We close by asking God to help each student to "not become weary in doing good."	Bibles, paper, poster-making supplies for art option (poster-board, markers, construction paper, magazines, glue, scissors), optional: evaluation forms from the back of this leader's guide	20-25 minutes

Note: **No student case studies or other handouts are needed for this session.**

SESSION BACKGROUND

For twelve weeks you've been teaching your students how to make good moral decisions. They've been learning about Christian ethics, about how we ought to act and live. During this final session we suggest that you encourage your students to actually *do* what they know they *ought* to do.

You may be wondering if such a reminder to do good is really necessary. Won't your students just do what they know they ought to do?

Perhaps. Perhaps not. Between *ought* and *do* there's a moral gap that leaves room for these questions: Are you sure this will work? Is it practical? And your students may realize that practicing a set of Christian ethics can, at times, actually hamper "success," at least as our society defines it. The question behind today's session is this: Does attempting to live by a Christian ethic actually work?

If pressed, some would say that Christ's teachings on how we ought to live are good ideals, but they are totally impractical in the real world. Take, for example, Jesus' well-known advice to turn the other cheek, to give someone your cloak if he takes your coat, to love your enemies (Matt. 5:39-40, 44). "Have you ever actually tried doing that?" these skeptics might ask. Turning the other cheek in some neighborhoods is inviting a second mugging. Giving away coats and cloaks, lending freely to the borrowing neighbor, is a fast track to bankruptcy. Hating an enemy is more natural and far better for your blood pressure than being nice to someone nasty. A Christian morality is attractive, these folks say, but, sadly, is unattainable for most of us who have to survive in a world that's far from ideal.

Others take the opposite view. If you're respectful, honest, upright, and hard-working, they say, you will succeed. Practicing Christian ethics is the key to career success. It's eminently practical. Morality works. God blesses the good. Believe, trust, do good—and win! Or, as someone once phrased it, "Get fat with faith."

Between these contrasting views is a third notion. Morality, ethics, loving enemies, turning the other cheek are fine, some suggest, within the Christian community and in private life. God expects us to love and do good there. But in our daily work, in sports, in politics, in our relationships with non-Christians, it's different. It's a dog-eat-dog world out there, and you have to be practical to survive and succeed. So you may have to cheat a little, cut some corners, pull some deals—that's understandable. As long as you show love and forgiveness when you can—usually among family, friends, and within the church community—God won't judge harshly. Christian ethics works just fine if you just keep it in its proper place.

Of course, all three views are false. None of them are "Christian" answers. In fact, the question itself is wrong. It's not important whether Christian ethical principles work or not—not in the sense of whether they help us succeed in this life—because God doesn't call us to succeed. God calls us to be disciples of Jesus Christ. This is not to say that living according to God's law isn't good for us—it is. But we don't obey the law because we want to be "successful." We obey it, first of all, because we love the One we're following.

That love motivates us to give Christ priority over everything else. It compels us to follow Christ, to be Christian in all our living. It keeps us going when we become weary and discouraged, when "doing the right thing" may actually hamper our "success." Love for Jesus makes obeying him something we want to do out of sheer gratitude for what he has done for us. It makes obedience a blessing, not a burden.

In the Sermon on the Mount, Jesus tells us how to live obediently in a way that shows our love for God and our neighbor. You could say that Jesus sharpened the Old Testament law on the whetstone of love. Live like this, Jesus is saying, and you will truly be blessed. Trust and obey, and you will enter the kingdom of God (Matt. 5:1-12).

Put another way, the ethical principles we've studied in this course are meant to guide our decisions and pattern our lives. They are meant to be lived out.

It's true, of course, that all of us will stumble and fall as we follow our Lord. Even Paul had to say that he had not "already been made perfect" (Phil. 3:12). Perfection comes only after death. But these principles do stake out the path that we should walk, a path that leads to a prize so glorious it staggers the imagination. "One thing I do," says Paul. "Forgetting what is behind and straining toward what is ahead, I press on toward the goal to win the prize for which God has called me heavenward in Christ Jesus" (Phil 3:13-14).

Encourage your students to walk the path of loving obedience, today and all of their lives. It's the only way to lasting joy and peace. It's the only "success" that really matters.

—HAS

LEADING THE SESSION

1 Review:
The Right Stuff
Materials: Bibles, newsprint, markers, masking tape

Begin by reminding the class that over the past ten weeks we've been applying the Ten Commandments to a variety of case studies. Explain that today we're going to return to take another look at the commandments and how we're doing on making them part of the way we try to live.

Divide into pairs, giving each pair a Bible, a sheet of newsprint, and a marker. Have the pairs turn to Exodus 20, then divide up the commandments among them. Ask the pairs to phrase the commandment is a way that's positive and that speaks to their lives. Allow up to ten minutes, depending on how many commandments each pair has been given.

TIP
If your group is very small, you may want students to work individually rather than in pairs.

---

activity adaptation

If some of your students enjoy sketching, give may want to give them the option of making drawings with captions to represent their assigned commandments.

Have the partners tape their newsprint sheets to the wall or display them on a table or floor. Comment that these are ten moral *oughts* that God gives us to live by. Have the pairs read their paraphrased commandments to the class.

Ask if anyone remembers how Jesus summarized the law. Have students turn to Matthew 22:34-40. Ask someone to read the passage aloud. Also have someone read Matthew 5:38-44, from Christ's Sermon on the Mount. Ask, **Do you think Jesus interpreted the Ten Commandments in a way that made them easier or harder to obey?**

Comment that Jesus' instructions for moral living often went beyond the Old Testament prohibitions, requiring us to act in loving ways that might seem unnatural and very challenging (loving enemies, turning the other cheek, and so on). As Harvey Smit says in the session background, "Jesus sharpened the Old Testament law on the whetstone of love."

2 Reflection and Discussion: The Right Reasons
Materials: Bibles, notecards (preferably 4" x 6"), pens

Give each student a notecard. Point to the paraphrased commandments and ask each person to select one statement that seems to be particularly helpful or relevant to him or her at this time. If students prefer, they may take a saying of Jesus from the Sermon on the Mount (Matt. 5-7).

Have each person copy the statement on the notecard. Then ask a question along these lines:

■ **What obstacles or difficulties might you face in actually trying to live out this ethical principle? Please jot your thoughts on the notecard.**

Ask for volunteers to read their cards to the class, including both the ethical principle they selected and the obstacles they might face in practicing that principle.

Take a moment to say that one common obstacle to living out these principles is the idea that they aren't very practical and could even cause a person some damage. Use Jesus' idea of loving your enemies as an example.

Point students to the truth that Jesus himself spelled out: if we want to follow Jesus, we can't expect smooth sailing, blessing after blessing with no problems. In fact, just the opposite is true: we may expect to suffer, to encounter difficulties and problems. To support this point, have someone read Luke 9:23 ("If anyone would come after me, he must deny himself and take up his cross daily and follow me").

Ask,

■ **In view of these obstacles, why would you want to try to live by this principle? Please jot your thoughts on the notecard.**

Again, invite volunteers to share their responses. Many answers are appropriate. A good response is that we obey because that's what Christ asks us to do as his followers—see, for example, John 14:15: "If you love me, you will obey what I command." But we also obey, as the verse from John spells out, because we love Jesus. It's our love for Jesus that makes us *want* to obey him. Out of gratitude for what he has done for us, we gladly obey him. What's more, this life of loving obedience may not bring us success and may even bring us some hurt, but it also brings lasting joy and peace, something that's worth far more than wealth and success.

Take a moment to have students find the Beatitudes in their Bibles (Matt. 5:3-12). Call attention to the string of blessings that Jesus promises those who follow him. Explain that the word "blessed" may be translated as "happy." The point is that the path of obedience is one that brings deep joy and lasting happiness into our lives. And it's a path that leads to heaven itself—not because of what we've done, but because of what God has done for us in Christ.

TIP

How do you give students a sense that the Holy Spirit breathes joy and happiness and peace and love into our lives when we obey Christ? Maybe one way is to tell something of the joy that you experience as you try to live a life of obedience. Or maybe you can ask your students to talk about the joy they experience as they live out their faith. Here's the thought you want to leave with students: **Living the Christian life is hard and challenging. But it is also exciting and surprising— and drenched in God's goodness. Doubt it? Try it!**

---

3 Presentations: Press On!

Materials: Bibles, paper, poster-making supplies for art option (posterboard, markers, construction paper, magazines, glue, scissors), optional: evaluation forms from the back of this leader guide

Comment that the apostle Paul is, among other things, a really great cheerleader who encourages us to keep the commandments and live in ways that are pleasing to God. Have students find Philippians 3:12-14 and ask someone to read it aloud. Comment that, like Paul, who also admitted that he was far from perfect, we need to "press on toward the goal to win the prize."

Divide all or some of the following "encouragement" passages from Paul among groups of two to four students each, one passage to a group (write the locations on newsprint or on your board):

- Galatians 6:9-10: "Let us not become weary in doing good . . ."

- Philippians 3:12-14: "I press on toward the goal to win the prize . . ."

- Philippians 4:13: "I can do everything through him who gives me strength."

- Romans 8:31-32: "If God is for us, who can be against us?"

TIP

Some of your students' responses may tilt toward the idea of the "success" gospel described in the session background. If so, take care to let them down gently, affirming that living according to God's commands does bring us real, lasting joy and that all good things come from God, but also explaining that we don't obey Christ in order to become rich or otherwise "succeed" in this world.

TIP

You may want to invite students to visualize the "prize" that Paul is talking about in Philippians 3:14. What, exactly, do they imagine this prize might be? If it's heaven, what do they think will be so great about getting there? Though your students are young and at the beginning of their journeys, remembering the prize that awaits them at the end can help get them through hard times that come their way.

- Romans 8:38-39: "[Nothing] will be able to separate us from the love of God . . ."

- 1 Corinthians 9:24-25: "Run in such a way as to get the prize . . ."

- Galatians 5:22: "But the fruit of the Spirit is love, joy, peace . . ."

Explain that the groups can decide how to present their passage to the class, in any way they think is interesting and effective.

---

activity adaptation

If groups are familiar with the Bible, you may want to give them the option of choosing their own passage of encouragement to present. Another beautiful passage, for example, is Isaiah 40:31 ("They will soar on wings like eagles, they will run and not grow weary . . ."). Another is John 14:1-4 ("I am going there to prepare a place for you").

Some possibilities for group presentations:

- Act out the action of the passage (this will work better with some of the passages than with others).

- Pantomime the passage, asking the class to guess what's being portrayed.

- Write a litany or rap based on the passage.

- Make a poster illustrating the passage, captioning it with a part of the passage.

Have your poster-making supplies handy for any group choosing to take that option. Allow about ten minutes for preparation, then have the groups present. At some point in their presentation, groups should read (aloud) the passage they've been given.

Ask students to look once more at the notecard used during step 2. Remind them that they chose this particular commandment or ethical principle as one that had particular relevance for their lives. Invite them to write (on the card) the location of one encouraging Scripture passage, a passage they can look up when discouraged about keeping that particular commandment or others. If there's room on the card, they may want to write a few words from that passage as a reminder.

Close by inviting students to form a tight circle. Ask one student to move to the center of the circle and have the rest of the group place their hands on this person's shoulders. As they do so, lead the class in saying in unison:

"Dear God, let [name of student] not become weary of doing good."

Repeat for each student.

118

activity adaptation: shortcut

If you're running out of time, skip the group presentations. Instead, have students read the "encouragement" passages aloud, then add a passage to their notecard and end with the prayer (see above).

Please note that we've included evaluation forms for you and your students at the back of this leader's guide. This is good time to complete these forms. Please mail the forms to the address found on the form. Thank you.

alternate session plan

Here's an outline of a plan that takes a somewhat different approach to today's session. No special materials are needed.

Step 1: Open by having pairs of students list three persons, dead or alive, that they consider to be successful. Do not define the word—just let students work with their own ideas of what it means. List names on newsprint or on your board. Then develop a list of reasons why students named these individuals as successful (for example, their accomplishments as athletes or musicians; their wealth; their influence on others; their exceptional kindness and love toward others; their modeling of the Christian life, and so on).

Step 2: Raise and discuss the question of what makes a Christian "successful." Explore the (false) notion that the only successful Christians are those whom God blesses with material possessions or power (see Session Background). Conclude together that a successful Christian is one who has been saved "by grace through faith," and who, in love and gratitude, seeks to live obediently as Jesus taught him or her to do, even though this obedience may cost a lot (see Luke 9:23).

Step 3: Read James 2:14-17 and ask students to (privately) rate themselves on how they are doing in living out their faith (1 = need lots of help; 10 = doing OK). Read Philippians 3:12-14 and notice how Paul admits he's far from perfect but he keeps pressing on.

Step 4: Have students use their Bibles to pick one of the commandments (or one of Jesus' statements from the Sermon on the Mount) and write an "action statement" based on that commandment, something he or she is willing to commit to doing in the next week. Have them jot a verse of encouragement beneath the action statement. Close with either silent prayer or partners praying for each other.

Resource Pages

For each session (except session 13) you'll be asked to photocopy a resource page and distribute it to your students. You'll find these resource pages in the section that follows. Each page is clearly labeled with a session number.

case study: stop or not?

You're driving alone on a lightly traveled highway, heading to your high school graduation. Your robe and cap are in the back seat of the car. You're mentally rehearsing your speech—as class president you've been asked to speak on behalf of the graduating class. You are a little nervous since you want to make a good impression on the hundreds of people who will be at the graduation ceremony in the school gym.

It's a nasty night in early June. At times the rain comes so fast and heavy that your wipers can hardly keep up. So you hold your speed down to a cautious 45, despite the fact that you're running a bit late. Suddenly, off to the right, you see taillights glowing upward at an impossible angle. You slow down, realizing that a car has skidded off the road into the ditch. From the road it's impossible to see if there's anyone inside.

Another driver passes you impatiently, laying on the horn. You wish you had a cell phone, but you don't. Do you stop and investigate? Do you risk ruining your clothes in the cold rain and missing your own graduation and speech? Or do you drive on?

For each of the following moral principles, ask yourself: *If I held this principle, would I stop or drive on? Why?*

1. *Glandular principle*
   If it feels good, do it. If not, why do it?

2. *Me-first principle*
   Looking out for number one. What's in it for me?

3. *Universal principle*
   Suppose everyone acted this way? What would our world be like?

4. *Golden Rule principle*
   How would I feel in that person's place?

5. *Conscience principle*
   An inner voice tells me what's right or wrong.

6. *Pass-the-buck principle*
   Let someone else do it.

7. *Good Samaritan principle*
   Love for my neighbor is the highest good.

8. *Legal principle*
   The law is always right. Do as you are told.

9. *Minimum risk principle.*
   How can I fulfill my obligation but at minimum risk to myself?

10. *Tradition principle*
    We've always done it this way.

11. *Sanctity of life principle*
    Human life is sacred, has top priority and claims

12. *WWJD*
    What would Jesus do in this situation?

FOR DISCUSSION

■ Do you have any other principles to add to this list—motives or attitudes that would help determine what we should do?

■ Give an example of how one moral principle could motivate different responses.

■ Do our moral principles influence the way we decide and act (a) a little (b) some (c) a lot (d) not at all? Why?

■ What do you think you might do if you were actually in that situation—stop, drive on, or something else? Why would you do it? What principle would influence you? (You may use a principle that's not on the list, if you wish.)

the *ought* of love

LOVE

What ideas about *love* are found in *all* of the following statements?

1. Teen to friend: "I really don't see anything wrong with sex before marriage—provided you really love each other and are going to get married anyway."

2. Student to police officer: "No, I'm not going to press charges. The guy who ripped out my car stereo has been caught before, I know, but this time he says he's really sorry. What's my Christianity worth if I only love those who love me?"

3. Teen to parent: "I don't want to hurt her feelings. She's my best friend, you know. I just can't tell her that what she's doing is cheating her employer. Our friendship would be over."

4. Teen to youth leader: "I can honestly say I love the poor people of our world. Pictures and stories about starving children make me cry. But I don't think that means I have to cut back on the way I live, the food I eat, the energy I use. I earned that. I'm willing to help, but not that way."

5. Teacher to student: "Sure, I know I said all term papers were due a week ago. And everyone made the deadline except you. And your only excuse is that you forgot. But, hey, no big deal. You're a good kid and it's good for me to show a little love and tolerance. So just hand in your paper as soon as you can, and I won't knock down your grade this time, OK?"

> **Ideas about love found in all these statements:**
>
>

LAW

What ideas about *law* (obedience) are found in *all* the following statements?

1. Dutchman to inquiring Nazi soldier: "I can't lie to you. There are Jews hiding in the house next door."

2. Pharisees to Jesus, who has just healed a man with a withered hand: "Is it lawful to heal on the Sabbath?"

3. Adult to friend: "We're way too soft on criminals. I say that anyone who murders—for any reason—should get the death penalty."

4. Parent to teen: "The church ought to think twice about taking him back. I mean, he's a youth worker, after all, and he got caught looking at porn on the Internet—right in his office in church! And now he expects us to take him back just because he says he's sorry! He should leave our church and get out of youth ministry. He's finished."

5. Teacher to student: "This term paper was due at 3:15 yesterday. I really don't want to hear your excuses. I have no choice but to knock you down a grade, just like I said I would for any paper that was a day late."

Ideas about law found in all these statements:

LOVE AND LAW: MAKING THE CONNECTION

Read John 14:15, Romans 13:8-10, and 1 John 5:3.

■ What do you think the *ought* of love refers to?

■ Try to write (in one sentence) what these passages teach us about the relationship between love and law.

LIVING YOUR LOVE

Think of one specific way that this idea of loving others—within the bounds of the law of God—could affect your attitude or actions toward someone in the coming week. Be practical—think of something you would actually be willing to do. Jot your response below.

God tells us
    to love our neighbor as ourselves,
    to be patient, peace-loving, gentle,
       merciful, and friendly to them,
    to protect them from harm as much as we can,
    and to do good even to our enemies.

—Heidelberg Catechism, Answer 107

first commandment

THE FIRST COMMANDMENT

And God spoke all these words: "I am the LORD your God, who brought you out of Egypt, out of the land of slavery. You shall have no other gods before me."

—Exodus 20:1-3

**What does the Lord require
in the first commandment?**

. . . That I sincerely acknowledge the only true God,
  trust him alone,
  look to him for every good thing
    humbly and patiently,
  love him, fear him, and honor him
  with all my heart.

—Heidelberg Catechism, Q&A 94

What is idolatry?

Idolatry is
  having or inventing something in which one trusts
  in place of or alongside of the only true God,
    who has revealed himself in his Word.

—Heidelberg Catechism, Q&A 95

"Whatever your heart clings to and confides in, that is your god."

— Martin Luther

"Christ told us that no one could serve two masters. It is either God or Money, not both. Every hobby, ideal, and possession is a potential idol. All of us must learn to put all of it in the service of our Lord and permit none of it to receive the devotion that is due to God alone."

— Andrew Kuyvenhoven

"For where your treasure is, there your heart will be also."

— Jesus (Matthew 6:21)

127

second commandment

THE SECOND COMMANDMENT

"You shall not make for yourself an idol in the form of anything in heaven above or on the earth beneath or in the waters below. You shall not bow down to them or worship them, for I, the LORD your God, am a jealous God, punishing the children for the sin of the fathers to the third and fourth generation of those who hate me, but showing love to a thousand generations of those who love me and keep my commandments."

—Exodus 20:4-6

**What is God's will for us
in the second commandment?**

That we in no way make any image of God
nor worship him in any other way
than he has commanded us in his Word.

—Heidelberg Catechism, Q&A 96

What does God look for when we worship? In other words, how can we worship in a way that pleases God? Draw on your own experiences and the passages and other material on this page. Jot your ideas here.

For the LORD is the great God,
   the great King above all gods. . . .
Come, let us bow down in worship
   let us kneel before the Lord our Maker.

—Psalm 95:3, 6

But we preach Christ crucified. . . .

—1 Corinthians 1:23

Simon Peter answered, "You are the Christ, the Son of the living God."

—Matthew 16:16

Our new life in Christ
is celebrated and nourished
in the fellowship of congregations
where God's name is praised,
his Word proclaimed,
his way taught;
where sins are confessed,
prayers and gifts are offered,
and sacraments are celebrated.

—*Our World Belongs to God,* stanza 39

To whom, then, will you compare God?
What image will you compare him to?
As for an idol, a craftsman casts it,
and a goldsmith overlays it with gold
and fashions silver chains for it.
A man too poor to present such an offering
selects wood that will not rot.
He looks for a skilled craftsman
to set up an idol that will not topple.
Do you not know?
Have you not heard?
Has it not been told you from the beginning?
Have you not understood since the earth was founded?
He sits enthroned above the circle of the earth,
and its people are like grasshoppers.
He stretches out the heavens like a canopy,
and spreads them out like a tent to live in.
He brings princes to naught
and reduces the rulers of this world to nothing.
No sooner are they planted,
no sooner are they sown,
no sooner do they take root in the ground,
than he blows on them and they wither,
and a whirlwind sweeps them away like chaff.
"To whom will you compare me?
Or who is my equal?" says the Holy One.

—Isaiah 40:18-25

"Yet a time is coming and has now come when the true worshipers will worship the Father in spirit and truth, for they are the kind of worshipers the Father seeks. God is spirit, and his worshipers must worship in spirit and in truth."

—John 4:23-24

And we have the word of the prophets made more certain, and you will do well to pay attention to it, as to a light shining in a dark place, until the day dawns and the morning star rises in your hearts.

—2 Peter 1:19

Consequently, faith comes from hearing the message, and the message is heard through the word of Christ.

—Romans 10:17

third commandment

THIRD COMMANDMENT LITANY

Group 1: You shall not misuse the name of the LORD your God, for the LORD will not hold anyone guiltless who misuses his name. *(Exodus 20:7)*

Group 2: What is God's will for us in the third commandment?

Group 1: That we use the holy name of God only with reverence and awe . . .

Group 2: so that we may properly confess him, pray to him, and praise him

All: in everything we do and say. *(Heidelberg Catechism, Q&A 99)*

Group 1: Why is God so concerned about God's name?

Group 2: God said, "This is my name forever, the name by which I am to be remembered from generation to generation." *(Exodus 3:15)*

Group 1: Not to us, O LORD, not to us but to your name be the glory, because of your love and faithfulness. *(Psalm 115:1)*

Group 2: Salvation is found in no one else, for there is no other name under heaven given to men by which we must be saved. *(Acts 4:12)*

Group 1: Therefore God exalted him to the highest place, and gave him the name that is above every name,

Group 2: that at the name of Jesus every knee should bow, in heaven and on earth and under the earth,

Group 1: and every tongue confess that Jesus Christ is Lord, to the glory of God the Father. *(Philippians 2:9-11)*

Group 2: Whatever you do, whether in word or deed, do it all in the name of the Lord Jesus, giving thanks to God the Father through him. *(Colossians 3:17)*

All: Dear God, help us to direct all our living—what we think, say, and do—so that your name will never be blasphemed because of us, but always honored and praised. *(Heidelberg Catechism, Answer 122)*

NEXT TIME YOU HEAR SOMEONE SWEAR . . .

Those who don't know the Father and his love in Jesus still use the name of God but merely as an expletive. When the man in the nice automobile got a scrape on his fender from a taxi that pulled up too close, the man got out of his vehicle and hollered, "Jesus Christ." And the taxi driver said, "Sir, why don't you call on someone you know."

—Andrew Kuyvenhoven, *Questions Worth Asking*

HOW DO YOU REACT TO PROFANITY?

- ■ It bothers me more when people I know use bad language, because I know they're good people and I expect better.

- ■ Bad language used to bother me a lot, but I've learned I can't give everybody a dirty look who uses it.

- ■ It makes me wince, but you can't talk to everybody who uses bad language or you'd never get to class on time.

—High school students

THIS SHOULD NOT BE

With the tongue we praise our Lord and Father, and with it we curse men, who have been made in God's likeness. Out of the same mouth come praise and cursing. . . . This should not be.

—James 3:9-10

fourth commandment

THE FOURTH COMMANDMENT

"Remember the Sabbath day by keeping it holy. Six days you shall labor and do all your work, but the seventh day is a Sabbath to the LORD your God. On it you shall not do any work, neither you, nor your son or daughter, nor your manservant or maidservant, nor your animals, nor the alien within your gates. For in six days the LORD made the heavens and the earth, the sea, and all that is in them, but he rested on the seventh day. Therefore the LORD blessed the Sabbath day and made it holy.

—Exodus 20:8-11

What is God's will for you in the fourth commandment?

That, especially on the festive day of rest,
I regularly attend the assembly of God's people. . . .

—Heidelberg Catechism, Q&A 103

THE ROAD FROM SABBATH TO SUNDAY

First Stop: Old Testament Israel

If you lived in Old Testament Israel, you would celebrate the Sabbath on the _____ day of the week because that was the day that God _____ from _____. The Sabbath was a joyful day set apart for God. On the Sabbath, you would get a much-needed break from all the normal _____ you did during the rest of the week. You would be expected to use the day to _____ (Leviticus 23:3). It would be a day not only to worship God and study the Torah, but also to be with your family, to rest, and to enjoy the good things God provided for you. For everyone in Israel, the Sabbath was not a gloomy day of many rules and regulations but a day of freedom and celebration.

Second Stop: Time of Jesus

Jesus himself observed the Sabbath by _____ (Luke 4:16). We know that he didn't do this every now and then but went faithfully, "as was his _____" (Luke 4:16). However, he often clashed with the Pharisees, who had managed to turn the Sabbath from a day of freedom and joyful celebration into a day of binding rules and regulations—some 1,521 of them in all, including one that prohibited tying a knot!

In Mark 2:23-27, the Pharisees accused Jesus of breaking their law against harvesting on the Sabbath. Jesus had violated this law, they claimed, by _____.
Jesus said that the Sabbath was made for people, not vice-versa. By this he meant that

_____.

Jesus also said that he was "Lord of the Sabbath" and had the authority to overrule _____ made by people about what could and could not be done on that day.

Third Stop: Early New Testament Church

If you were a Christian—either Jewish or Gentile—living during the time of the early New Testament church, you and other Christians would find yourself worshiping not on the last day of the week but on the first. Why? Because the first day of the week marked the _____ (Matthew 28:1) of your Lord and the beginning of new life. Like the original Sabbath for Old Testament Israel, Sunday for you would be a day of victorious celebration and freedom, a day of freedom from weekly routines but also a holy day, the Lord's Day.

Fourth Stop: Today

For Christians today, Sunday—the Lord's Day—should not be a gloomy day of numerous prohibitions—"don't do this; don't do that." Christ has renewed it, restored its original moral meaning, and made it the day of victory.

So how does God want us to spend our Sundays? How can be best make this day a separate day, a holy day? Read Mark 2:27-28; Mark 3:1-5; and Hebrews 10:24-25; and then list three guidelines for the Lord's Day. If you wish, add other guidelines that help you make the Lord's Day a special day.

1. _____

2. _____

3. _____

fifth commandment

THE FIFTH COMMANDMENT

"Honor your father and your mother, so that you may live long in the land the LORD your God is giving you."

—Exodus 20:12

What is God's will for you in the fifth commandment?

That I honor, love, and be loyal to
my father and mother
and all those in authority over me;
that I obey and submit to them, as is proper,
when they correct and punish me;
and also that I be patient with their failings—
for through them God chooses to rule us.

—Heidelberg Catechism, Q&A 104

Children, obey your parents in the Lord, for this is right. "Honor your father and mother"—which is the first commandment with a promise—"that it may go well with you and that you may enjoy long life on the earth."

Fathers, do not exasperate your children; instead, bring them up in the training and instruction of the Lord.

—Ephesians 6:1-4

Everyone must submit himself to the governing authorities, for there is no authority except that which God has established.

—Romans 13:1

Listen to your father, who gave you life,
    and do not despise your mother
        when she is old.

—Proverbs 23:22

"I don't feel too good about the idea that I should be patient with my parents' failings. When they do something wrong, I'm like, 'Aha! Now look what you did.'"

—High school student

135

Just yesterday I saw a new TV commercial, a public service announcement that didn't sell shampoo or gym shoes or some life-changing dot.com. The only visual image for a whole minute was a baby. The voice-over laid out the pitch. I can't quote it exactly, but it went something like this: "Today this little boy's father left the family. When he did, he increased this baby's chances of never finishing high school, of having a drug problem, of living a life of crime . . ." Then the commercial took aim at fathers. "If you leave home," it said, "don't neglect your children. Support your kids and encourage them, because children need your love far more than anything from Toys-R-Us."

—James C. Schaap, *Every Bit of Who I Am: Devotions for Teens,*
CRC Publications, Fleming H. Revell

Like their children, parents are not perfect. They are themselves still beginners in the art of Christian living. They get angry over the wrong things. They forget their task as Christian mothers and fathers, lose sight of God, and get all caught up in little pointless matters. Yet it is crucial that parents try to live the kind of lives they want their children to live. If a mother warns her children, "Don't lie," but thinks nothing of canceling an appointment with a false, "Sorry, I'm sick," they will learn that lying is all right when convenient. . . . Parents must remember that almost everything they say and do influences their children.

—Jack Roeda, *Decisions,* CRC Publications

Sometimes honoring father and mother means giving in, not because they're right and you're wrong but because we have much bigger obligations. The fifth commandment doesn't require us to honor our parents because it's such a sweet thing to do. It's a directive from God's Supreme Court; God says it's right. We honor God by honoring our parents, and we dishonor God by dishonoring them. That raises the stakes.

—James C. Schaap, *Every Bit of Who I Am: Devotions for Teens,*
CRC Publications, Fleming H. Revell

sixth commandment

THE SIXTH COMMANDMENT

"You shall not murder."

—Exodus 20:13

What is God's will for you in the sixth commandment?

I am not to belittle, insult, hate, or kill my neighbor
    not by my thoughts, my words, my look or gesture
    and certainly not by actual deeds—
and I am not to be party to this in others;
rather, I am to put away all desire for revenge.

I am not to harm or recklessly endanger myself either.

Prevention of murder is also why
    government is armed with the sword.

—Heidelberg Catechism, Q&A 105

No matter what our age, or race, or color
we are the human family together,
for the Creator made us all.
Since life is his gift,
we foster the well-being of others,
protecting the unborn and helpless from harm.

—*Our World Belongs to God,* stanza 12

Then God said, "Let us make man in our image, in our likeness. . . ." So God created man in his own image, in the image of God he created him, male and female he created them.

—Genesis 1:26-27

You gave me life and showed me kindness. . . .

—Job 10:12

You made [humankind] a little lower than the heavenly beings
    and crowned him with glory and honor.
You made him ruler over the works of your hands;
    you put everything under his feet.

—Psalm 8:5-6

137

Your hands have made me and formed me. . . .

—Psalm 119:73

You created my inmost being;
you knit me together in my mother's womb.
I praise you because I am fearfully and wonderfully made.

—Psalm 139:13-14

"I have made you and I will carry you;
I will sustain you and I will rescue you."

—Isaiah 46:4

Through [Christ] all things were made; without him nothing was made that has been made. In him was life, and that life was the light of men.

—John 1:3-4

For God so loved the world that he gave his one and only Son, that whoever believes in him shall not perish but have eternal life.

—John 3:16

You are not your own; you were bought with a price.

—1 Corinthians 6:20

ADDITIONAL PASSAGES FOR THE CASE STUDIES

"Whoever sheds the blood of man,
   by man shall his blood be shed;
for in the image of God
   has God made man."

—Genesis 9:6

"Put your sword back in its place," Jesus said, "for all who draw the sword will die by the sword."

—Matthew 26:52

Be merciful, just as your Father is merciful.

—Luke 6:36

Do you want to be free from fear of the one in authority? Then do what is right and he will commend you. For he is God's servant to do you good. But if you do wrong, be afraid, for he does not bear the sword for nothing.

—Romans 13:3-4

Don't show favoritism. . . . Has not God chosen those who are poor in the eyes of the world to be rich in faith and to inherit the kingdom he promised those who love him? . . . If you really keep the royal law found in Scripture, "Love your neighbor as yourself," you are doing right. But if you show favoritism, you sin. . . . Speak and act as those who are going to be judged by the law that gives freedom, because judgment without mercy will be shown to anyone who has not been merciful. Mercy triumphs over judgment!

—James 2:1, 5, 8-9, 12-13

The King will reply, "I tell you the truth, whatever you did for one of the least of these brothers of mine, you did for me."

—Matthew 25:40

seventh commandment

THE SEVENTH COMMANDMENT

"You shall not commit adultery."

—Exodus 20:14

What is God's will for us in the seventh commandment?

God condemns all unchastity.
   We should therefore thoroughly detest it
   and, married or single,
   live decent and chaste lives.

—Heidelberg Catechism, Q&A 108

Does God, in this commandment, forbid only such scandalous sins as adultery?

We are temples of the Holy Spirit, body and soul,
and God wants both to be kept clean and holy.
That is why he forbids
   everything which incites unchastity,
     whether it be actions, looks, talk, thoughts, or desires.

—Heidelberg Catechism, Q&A 109

Since God made us male and female in his image,
one sex may not look down on the other,
nor should we flaunt or exploit our sexuality.
Our roles as men and women must conform
to God's gifts and commands
as we shape our cultural patterns.
Sexuality is distorted in our fallen world;
grief and loneliness are the result;
but Christ's renewing work gives hope
for order and healing
and surrounds suffering persons
with a compassionate community.

—*Our World Belongs to God,* stanza 47

So God created man in his own image,
    in the image of God he created him;
    male and female he created him.
God blessed them and said to them, "Be fruitful and increase in number; fill the earth and subdue it. . . .
God saw all that he had made, and it was very good.

—Genesis 1:27-28, 31

"Christianity is almost the only one of the great religions which thoroughly approves of the body . . . and nearly all the greatest love poetry in the world has been produced by Christians."

—C. S. Lewis, *Mere Christianity*

Do you not know that your body is a temple of the Holy Spirit, who is in you, whom you have received from God? You are not your own; you were bought at a price. Therefore honor God with your body.

—1 Corinthians 6:19-20

But among you there must not be even a hint of sexual immorality, or any kind of impurity, or of greed, because these are improper for God's holy people. Nor should there be obscenity, foolish talk or coarse joking, which are out of place, but rather thanksgiving.

—Ephesians 5:3-4

"Whoever welcomes a little child like this in my name welcomes me. But if anyone causes one of these little ones who believe in me to sin, it would be better for him to have a large millstone hung around his neck and to be drowned in the depths of the sea."

—Matthew 18:5-6

And the LORD God commanded the man, "You are free to eat from any tree in the garden; but you must not eat from the tree of the knowledge of good and evil, for when you eat of it you will surely die."

—Genesis 2:16-17

Everyone must submit himself to the governing authorities, for there is no authority except that which God has established. The authorities that exist have been established by God.

—Romans 13:1

Love is patient, love is kind. It does not envy, it does not boast, it is not proud. It is not rude, it is not self-seeking, it is not easily angered, it keeps no records of wrongs. Love does not delight in evil but rejoices with the truth. It always protects, always trusts, always hopes, always perseveres. . . . And now, these three remain: faith, hope and love. But the greatest of these is love.

—1 Corinthians 13:4-7, 13

PASSAGES FOR ALTERNATE CASE STUDY: "GO LIVE WITH YOUR MISTRESS"

If a man has recently married, he must not be sent to war or have any other duty laid on him. For one year he is to be free to stay at home and bring happiness to the wife he has married.

—Deuteronomy 24:5

Wives, submit to your husbands, as is fitting in the Lord.
Husbands, love your wives and do not be harsh with them.
Children, obey your parents in everything, for this pleases the Lord.
Fathers, do not embitter your children, or they will become discouraged. . . .
Whatever you do, work at it with your whole heart, as working for the Lord, not for men.

—Colossians 3:18-21, 23

Each of you also must love his wife as he loves himself, and the wife must respect her husband.

—Ephesians 5:33

eighth commandment

THE EIGHTH COMMANDMENT

"You shall not steal."

—Exodus 20:15

What does God forbid in the eighth commandment?

He forbids not only outright theft and robbery,
punishable by law.

But in God's sight theft also includes
   cheating and swindling our neighbor
   by schemes made to appear legitimate,
   such as:
      inaccurate measurements of weight, size,
        or volume;
      fraudulent merchandising;
      counterfeit money;
      excessive interest;
      or any other means forbidden by God.

In addition he forbids all greed
and pointless squandering of his gifts.

—Heidelberg Catechism, Q&A 110

What does God require of you in this commandment?

That I do whatever I can
   for my neighbor's good,
that I treat others
   as I would like them to treat me,
and that I work faithfully
   so that I may share with those in need.

—Heidelberg Catechism, Q&A 111

The earth is the Lord's, and everything in it, the world, and all who live in it.

—Psalm 24:1

"So in everything, do to others what you would have them do to you, for this sums up the Law and the Prophets."

—Matthew 7:12

"Whoever can be trusted with very little can also be trusted with much, and whoever is dishonest with very little will also be dishonest with much."

—Luke 16:10

He who has been stealing must steal no longer, but must work, doing something useful with his own hands, that he may have something to share with those in need.

—Ephesians 4:28

"Don't be deceived by the simplicity of the Ten Commandments. "You shall not steal" sounds like a no-brainer, but life itself . . . can overflow with greed, the love of *stuff*. Stealing isn't just grabbing a CD from a Wal-Mart. We steal because we love stuff— just got to have it."

—James C. Schaap, *Every Bit of Who I Am: Devotions for Teens,*
CRC Publications, Fleming H. Revell

THE PARABLE OF THE RICH FOOL

Someone in the crowd said to him, "Teacher, tell my brother to divide the inheritance with me."

Jesus replied, "Man, who appointed me a judge or an arbiter between you?" Then he said to them, "Watch out! Be on your guard against all kinds of greed; a man's life does not consist in the abundance of his possessions."

And he told them this parable: "The ground of a certain rich man produced a good crop. He thought to himself, 'What shall I do? I have no place to store my crops.'

"Then he said, 'This is what I'll do. I will tear down my barns and build bigger ones, and there I will store all my grain and my goods. And I'll say to myself, "You have plenty of good things laid up for many years. Take life easy; eat, drink, and be merry."'

"But God said to him, 'You fool! This very night your life will be demanded from you. Then who will get what you have prepared for yourself?'

"This is how it will be with anyone who stores up things for himself but is not rich toward God."

—Luke 12:13-21

THE PARABLE OF THE RICH KID

Use your imagination to fill in the blanks.

Once there was a certain rich kid who, just one year out of high school, had invented a

_____ and struck it rich. The money from

the invention bought a fantastic place to live that was located on _____ and

featured, among other things, _____

and _____. The rich kid's possessions included a

couple of rare _____, a _____ full of _____,

more _____ than he/she could count, and, most valuable of all, a

_____.

One day, after a bigger-than-usual spending spree at _____, the rich

kid realized that there was a problem: _____

_____

_____.

"I know how to fix this!" the rich kid thought. "I'll just _____

_____. Then I'll say to myself, 'You know what?

You_____

_____.'"

But the rich kid was forgetting something. That very night he/she was _____

when _____ and _____.

All the stuff owned by the rich kid was _____!

The lesson of our little story is this:_____

_____.

ninth commandment

THE NINTH COMMANDMENT

"You shall not give false testimony against your neighbor."

—Exodus 20:16

SURVEY: THE LIES WE TELL

Rank the following examples of lies, from the most offensive (1) to the least offensive. You may fill in an example of your own to rank, if you wish.

____ Telling a friend you love her new haircut when, in fact, you think it's a total disaster.

____ Telling your teacher your kid sister blew away your term paper file on the computer, and that's why it's late (when in fact you simply needed more time to finish).

____ Telling a boyfriend/girlfriend that you're not seeing someone else, when you really are.

____ Telling your teacher that a term paper is all your own work, when in fact you copied most of it off the Internet without acknowledging your sources.

____ Lying to protect a friend from getting into trouble because of his or her drug problem.

____ Spreading a vicious and false rumor about someone you dislike.

____ Lying to parents so you can go out with your friends.

____ Remaining silent when you know who vandalized the school last night.

____ Lying in a court of law.

____ Making up an untrue excuse to avoid going out with someone you don't like.

____ Other:

____ Other:

MORE ON THE NINTH COMMANDMENT

The LORD detests lying lips,
but he delights in [those] who are truthful.

—Proverbs 12:22

Do not lie to each other, since you have taken off your old self with its practices and have put on the new self, which is being renewed in knowledge in the image of its Creator.

—Colossians 3:9

147

Instead, speaking the truth in love, we will in all things grow up into him who is the Head, that is, Christ.

—Ephesians 4:15

Jesus answered, "I am the way and the truth and the life."

—John 14:6

And I will ask the Father, and he will give you another Counselor to be with you forever— the Spirit of truth. The world cannot accept him, because it neither sees him or knows him. But you know him, for he lives with you and will be in you.

—John 14:16-17

What is God's will for you in the ninth commandment?

God's will is that I
   never give false testimony against anyone,
   twist no one's words,
   not gossip or slander,
   nor join in condemning anyone
   without a hearing or without a just cause.

Rather, in court and everywhere else,
I should avoid lying and deceit of every kind;
   these are devices the devil himself uses,
   and they would call down on me God's intense anger.
I should love the truth,
   speak it candidly,
   and openly acknowledge it.
And I should do what I can
   to guard and advance my neighbor's good name.

—Heidelberg Catechism, Q&A 112

ANANIAS AND SAPPHIRA

The whole congregation of believers was united as one—one heart, one mind! They didn't even claim ownership of their own possessions. No one said, "That's mine; you can't have it." They shared everything. The apostles gave powerful witness to the resurrection of the Master Jesus, and grace was on all of them.

And so it turned out that not a person among them was needy. Those who owned fields or houses sold them and brought the price of the sale to the apostles and made an offering of it. The apostles then distributed it according to each person's need.

Joseph, called by the apostles "Barnabas" (which means "Son of Comfort"), a Levite born in Cyprus, sold a field that he owned, brought the money and made an offering of it to the apostles.

But a man named Ananias—his wife, Sapphira, conniving in this with him—sold a piece of land, secretly kept part of the price for himself, and then brought the rest to the apostles and made an offering of it.

Peter said, "Ananias, how did Satan get you to lie to the Holy Spirit and secretly keep back part of the price of the field? Before you sold it, it was all yours, and after you sold it, the money was yours to do with as you wished. So what got into you to pull a trick like this? You didn't lie to men but to God."

Ananias, when he heard these words, fell down dead. *That* put the fear of the God into everyone who heard of it. The younger men went right to work and wrapped him up, then carried him out and buried him.

Not more than three hours later, his wife, knowing nothing of what had happened, came in. Peter said, "Tell me, were you given this price for your field?"

"Yes," she said, "that price."

Peter responded, "What's going on here that you connived to conspire against the Spirit of the Master? The men who buried your husband are at the door, and you're next." No sooner were the words out of his mouth than she also fell down, dead. When the young men returned they found her body. They carried her out and buried her beside her husband.

By this time the whole church and, in fact, everyone who heard of these things

_____

_____

_____.

—Acts 4:32-5:11, *The Message.* Used by permission.

tenth commandment

THE TENTH COMMANDMENT

"You shall not covet your neighbor's house. You shall not covet your neighbor's wife, or his manservant or maidservant, his ox or donkey, or anything that belongs to your neighbor."

—Exodus 20:17

BIBLE STUDY: COVETING VERSUS CONTENTMENT

One Man's Envy (1 Kings 21)

Narrator 1: Some time later there was an incident involving a vineyard belonging to Naboth, the Jezreelite. The vineyard was in Jezreel, close to the palace of Ahab king of Samaria.

Ahab: Naboth, let me have your vineyard to use for a vegetable garden, since it is close to my palace. In exchange, I will pay you whatever it's worth.

Naboth: The Lord forbid that I should give you the inheritance of my fathers.

Narrator 2: So Abraham went home, sullen and angry because Naboth the Jezreelite had said, "I will not give you the inheritance of my fathers." He lay on his bed sulking and refused to eat.

Jezebel: Why are you so sullen? Why won't you eat?

Ahab: Because I said to Naboth the Jezreelite, "Sell me your vineyard; or if you prefer, I will give you another vineyard in its place." But he said, "I will not give you my vineyard."

Jezebel: Is this how you act as king over Israel? Get up and eat! Cheer up. I'll get you the vineyard of Naboth the Jezreelite.

Narrator 1: So she wrote letters in Ahab's name, placed his seal on them, and sent them to the elders and nobles who lived in Naboth's city with him. In those letters she wrote,

Jezebel: "Proclaim a day of fasting and seat Naboth in a prominent place among the people. But seat two scoundrels opposite him and have them testify that he has cursed both God and the king. Then take him out and stone him to death."

Narrator 2: So the elders and nobles who lived in Naboth's city did as Jezebel directed in the letters she had written to them. They proclaimed a fast and seated Naboth in a prominent place among the people. Then two scoundrels came and sat opposite him and brought charges against Naboth before the people.

Scoundrels: Naboth has cursed God and the king!

Narrator 1: So they took him outside the city and stoned him to death. Then they sent word to Jezebel: "Naboth has been stoned and is dead."

Narrator 2: As soon as Jezebel heard that Naboth had been stoned to death, she said to Ahab,

Jezebel: Get up and take possession of the vineyard of Naboth the Jezreelite that he refused to sell you. He is no longer alive, but dead.

Narrator 1: When Ahab heard that Naboth was dead, he got up and went down to take possession of Naboth's vineyard.

Narrator 2: Then the word of the LORD came to Elijah the Tishbite.

The Lord: Go down to meet Ahab king of Israel, who rules in Samaria. He is now in Naboth's vineyard, where he has gone to take possession of it. Say to him, "This is what the LORD says: 'Have you not murdered a man and seized his property?'" Then say to him, "This is what the LORD says, 'In the place where dogs licked up Naboth's blood, dogs will lick up your blood—yes, yours!'"

Ahab: So, Elijah, you have found me, my enemy!

Elijah: I have found you because you have sold yourself to do evil in the eyes of the LORD. "I am going to bring disaster on you," says the LORD. "I will consume your descendants and cut off from Ahab every last male in Israel—slave or free." And also concerning Jezebel, the LORD says, "Dogs will devour Jezebel by the wall of Jezreel."

Narrator 1: (There was never a man like Ahab, who sold himself to do evil in the sight of the LORD, urged on by Jezebel his wife.)

Narrator 2: When Ahab heard these words, he tore his clothes, put on sackcloth and fasted. He lay in sackcloth and went around meekly.

The Lord (to Elijah): Have you noticed how Ahab has humbled himself before me? Because he has humbled himself, I will not bring this disaster in his day, but I will bring it on his house in the days of his son.

■ How would you classify Ahab's case of coveting: mild or severe? Why?

■ Imagine yourself as Ahab. You are defending your coveting and the action you took. What would you say?

■ What can we learn about coveting from this story?

■ What can we learn about God from this story?

One Man's Contentment

Five times I received from the Jews the forty lashes minus one. Three times I was beaten with rods, once I was stoned, three times I was shipwrecked, I spent a night and a day in the open sea, I have been constantly on the move.

I have been in danger from rivers,
    in danger from bandits,
    in danger from my own countrymen,
    in danger from Gentiles;
    in danger in the city,
    in danger in the country,
    in danger at sea;
    and in danger from false brothers.
I have labored and toiled and have often gone without sleep;
I have known hunger and thirst and have often gone without food;
I have been cold and naked.
Besides everything else, I face daily the pressures of my concern for all the churches. Who
    is weak, and I do not feel weak? Who is led into sin, and I do not inwardly burn?
                                                    —Paul, 2 Corinthians 11:24-29

I have learned the secret of being content in any and every situation. . . . I can do everything through him who gives me strength.
                                                    —Paul, Philippians 4:12-13

■ If you were in Paul's shoes, what would you be tempted to covet?

■ Unlike Ahab, who is discontented with much, Paul seems content with very little. What's his secret?

■ What helps you resist coveting and be content with what God has given you?

Leader

evaluation form: *no easy answers*

1. Overall, I rate this course as

   (a) excellent
   (b) good
   (c) fair
   (d) poor

2. In general, I found the case study method to be

   (a) a helpful way to teach Christian ethics
   (b) an ineffective way to teach Christian ethics.

3. Some case studies I found especially helpful are (please list by title or describe):

4. Some case studies that should be updated or dropped are (please list by title or describe):

5. One suggestion I have for improving this course is:

Name (optional): _____

Church: _____

Age group taught: _____

Size of class: _____

Amount of time for each class session:_____

Thank you!

Please send all comments to

No Easy Answers
Faith Alive Christian Resources
2850 Kalamazoo Ave SE
Grand Rapids, MI 49560

Student

evaluation form: *no easy answers*

1. Overall, I rate this course as

   (a) excellent
   (b) good
   (c) fair
   (d) poor

2. On a scale of 1 (poor) to 10 (excellent), I rate the case studies used in this course as _____.

3. Some case studies I found especially helpful are (please list by title or describe the case):

4. Some case studies that should be updated or dropped are (please list by title or describe):

5. One thing I learned from this course is:

6. One suggestion I have for improving this course is:

Name (optional): _____

Church: _____

School grade:_____

Gender: _____

Thank you!

Please send all comments to

No Easy Answers
Faith Alive Christian Resources
2850 Kalamazoo Ave SE
Grand Rapids, MI 49560